Fantastic Families

Fantastic Families

6 Proven Steps
to Building
a Strong Family

DR. NICK & NANCY STINNETT
JOE & ALICE BEAM

HOWARD
PUBLISHING CO.

Our purpose at Howard Publishing is to:
- *Increase faith* in the hearts of growing Christians
- *Inspire holiness* in the lives of believers
- *Instill hope* in the hearts of struggling people everywhere
Because He's coming again!

Fantastic Families © 1999 by Dr. Nick & Nancy Stinnett and Joe & Alice Beam
All rights reserved. Printed in the United States of America

Published by Howard Publishing Co., Inc.,
3117 North 7th Street, West Monroe, Louisiana 71291-2227

99 00 01 02 03 04 05 06 07 08   10 9 8 7 6 5 4 3 2 1

Library of Congress Cataloging-in-Publication Data
Fantastic families : 6 proven steps to building a strong family / Nick Stinnett ... [et al.].
    p. cm.
   Includes bibliographical references.
   ISBN 1-58229-080-6
    1. Family—United States. 2. Interpersonal relations—United States.
   3. Communication—United States.   I. Stinnett, Nick.
   HQ535.F355   1999
   306.85'0973—dc21   99-39750
                                                   CIP

Edited by Philis Boultinghouse
Interior design by Stephanie Denney
Cover design by LinDee Loveland

Publisher's Note: Because everyone's particular situation is unique, the ideas and suggestions contained in this book should not be considered a substitute for consultation with a psychiatrist or trained therapist.

Scripture quotations not otherwise marked are from the Holy Bible, New International Version. Copyright © 1973, 1978, 1984 International Bible Society. Used by permission of Zondervan Bible Publishers. Other Scriptures are quoted from The Holy Bible, Authorized King James Version (KJV), © 1961 by The National Publishing Co.; the American Standard Edition of the Revised Version (ASV), © 1929 by International Council of Religious Education; The Holy Bible, New King James Version (NKJV), © 1982 by Thomas Nelson, Inc. All rights reserved.

Dedicated with love
to our families and friends
and with gratitude
to the families of the
Family-Strengths Research Project.

◆ CONTENTS ◆

Editorial Note: You hold in your hands the result of a twenty-five-year research project that studied fourteen thousand families around the world. No other study has ever looked at this many strong families over this many years. With the information in this book, you can take the guesswork out of building a healthy family and focus your energy and efforts on what really works. It is the prayer of all who worked to bring you this valuable information that you and your family become all that you can be—a *fantastic family!*

SOME THINGS YOU NEED TO KNOW

ABOUT THE RESEARCHERS AND AUTHORS

The research that forms the foundation of this book began twenty-five years ago on an automobile trip across the rolling hills of Oklahoma and the abundant prairies of western Texas. Nick and Nancy Stinnett were traveling from their home in Stillwater, Oklahoma, to Lubbock, Texas. The drive across western Oklahoma and the panhandle of Texas is long with small towns scattered miles apart. The interstate highway is flat, straight, and easy to drive, which allows for a lot of conversation. As Nick and Nancy conversed, their thoughts turned to some of the prevailing issues of the time: Divorce rates were soaring, more women were entering the work force, and family violence was increasing. They discussed the consensus held in many circles that the family was dead—or at least dying. But Nick and Nancy weren't willing to accept this disturbing conclusion. They believed that there were many families who weren't falling apart, who were actually doing quite well. Nick and Nancy wanted to know: What were these families like? What made them different?

As soon as they returned to Stillwater, Nick began a search for families that were doing well. Rather than taking the approach, "Let's find out what's wrong with families," Nick decided to pursue the characteristics of successful families. What is it that families are doing right that makes them strong and happy and keeps them functioning correctly?

Nick quickly realized that a variety of terms could be used when describing families that are living and working well: successful, balanced, healthy, functional, good, strong. He decided to primarily use the word *strong* in describing these families because the term is clear, straightforward, and positive.

Nick began the study in 1974 with a group of graduate students, and Dr. John DeFrain joined the research in 1977. This quest began over twenty-five years ago, and at this writing, approximately fourteen thousand families have formally contributed to this research through interviews, observations, and by filling out questionnaires. These families represent all fifty states and twenty-four countries around the world. At last count, about forty master's theses and doctoral dissertations have been written on family strengths by members of this team of colleagues. In all, about fifty researchers have been involved in the studies over the years. (If you wish to know more about how the research was conducted, see Appendix D.)

Nick Stinnett and John DeFrain have discussed the family-strengths principles in numerous professional journals, popular magazine articles, newspapers, and books; on radio and television programs; and in seminars and workshops throughout the nation. When it came time for them to publish their discoveries in book form, Nick asked his friend Joe Beam to contribute his insight into what Scripture says about the principles they'd discovered and to share applicable stories from the thousands of marriages he works with through Family Dynamics Institute.

The researchers (primarily Stinnett and DeFrain) and the authors of this book bring a variety of perspectives and experience to the table and are thus able to approach the question of how to develop strong families from several directions. Nick and Nancy Stinnett (University of Alabama, Tuscaloosa) and John and Nikki DeFrain (University of

Nebraska, Lincoln) are teachers, internationally recognized researchers, family counselors and educators, and family members. Joe and Alice Beam are the founders of Family Dynamics Institute, a non-profit corporation that leads thousands of couples through interactive marriage seminars or parenting seminars each year.

As researchers with a painful knowledge of the sad statistics on family problems, they have to agree that many families are in trouble today. Their own studies of divorce, violence, and death in families show the tremendous need for help that literally millions of families have. And through counseling people in trouble on a regular basis, they are profoundly aware of how family troubles can be the root of despair, madness, and even death.

Added together, they have many years of formal and informal experience in counseling. And although none of them counsels on a full-time basis (because of research and teaching responsibilities), they have heard just about everything. As professionals, they have been in the middle of most every kind of family woe imaginable: child and spouse abuse, incest, child custody battles, suicide, alcohol and drug abuse, and infidelity.

But the thousands of strong families in this research have shown that families can also bring out the best in humans. They teach us about the joy, pride, satisfaction, and pleasure that families can bring. They convince us that there are millions of good families across our nation and around the world.

ABOUT THE "FAMILY QUOTES" AND STORIES

All of the stories in this book are based on real people and real events, but unless a person's first *and* last names are used, the people, places, and events may have been disguised to protect privacy. In some instances two or more stories have been combined into one composite. In all cases, however, the many quotes from strong families represent accurately what they said and what they've learned about family life.

Since the research by Drs. Stinnett and DeFrain involved more than the Christian community (people of all kinds of religious beliefs and heritages were studied), it's possible that some of the views expressed by the families may differ from your own. Please don't let the view of any single family distract you from the value of this information. After all, most of the world's major religions cherish the family unit and hold to very similar beliefs about its sanctity and survival.

The fact that people from such a wide variety of backgrounds were included means that the findings of this research are universal. It means that any family on planet Earth can be strong if they apply these six characteristics to their family life.

READING THIS BOOK TOGETHER AS A FAMILY

This book has been designed so that you and your children may read it together, if you wish. While the material is written in an easy-to-read style, the concepts and information are up-to-date and in line with the highly recognized research of Stinnett and DeFrain.

Joe Beam's Family Dynamics Institute has designed a special interactive course for families based on this book and an accompanying study guide. The course helps families make the six secrets of successful families gleaned from Stinnett and DeFrain's research a vital and vibrant part of their own families.[1]

One last word about this book and children. Some of the stories—especially about husbands and wives—may be a little too intense for children. If you read this book to your children or with your children, please preview each chapter and decide what information, if any, you may wish to "edit" for your children's sake. Your whole family will benefit from this study, but you, the parent, must decide how to share each of the concepts with your children as you work to make your family all that it can be.

May the knowledge and wisdom shared in this book bless your life and your family and help you build a *fantastic family!*

WHAT MAKES A FAMILY STRONG, HEALTHY, AND HAPPY?

W hen something like that happens to you, you're never the same." Ed began his story calmly, but you could see in his eyes that he relived some of its terror as he remembered the night his life changed. "Amazing, isn't it? Just like that, the things that used to be important no longer are, and what took second place in your life just hours before suddenly becomes the only reason you want to live.

"We must have been thirty thousand feet or higher on our flight to Chicago, but even being that high above my problems didn't help. I was in trouble—serious trouble—and I was going to have to face it all when I landed in Chicago. The president of our company had summoned me, and I could imagine what that meeting was going to be like. Things had *not* been going well in the business—particularly in my region of the nation. Most of the problems were related to the economy—which meant they were beyond my control—but I was the boss in my region, and that made me the one accountable. While I believed most of our difficulties were temporary, I wasn't sure I could convince the president."

He shifted uncomfortably, worried that he wasn't being understood. "You see, while riding on that plane, all I could think about was that I might be fired the next day—out of work in middle age. Work had been so important to me for so many years that I had sacrificed many things to get ahead and succeed in business. I'm ashamed to say it, but I'd neglected my wife and children in order to climb the corporate ladder. And there I was, flying to a meeting in which the ladder I'd given my life to climb might be pulled right out from under me. That fear was the whole focus of my life at that moment.

"A moment later, everything changed.

"Suddenly the plane began to rock and bump, and then, without warning, it just fell. That's right; it just dropped like a rock. A flight attendant hurrying past me actually left the floor, throwing her hands above her head to keep from hitting her head on the ceiling. It must have been only a second or two, but it seemed like an eternity before the plane jarred as if it had hit a concrete wall and then, mercifully, resumed flying, continuing to bump and sway erratically.

"It was almost like some *Twilight Zone* episode. Just five minutes ago, we had been flying in moonlight and stars, and now we were engulfed in extremely rough weather. Lightning flashed around us, and thunder crashed deafeningly through the plane as flight attendants scurried down each aisle to see if anyone was hurt. They didn't get far before a passenger screamed that one of the engines was on fire!

"I've never been so scared. Panicked thoughts rushed unchecked through my terrified brain—things like, 'We're going to crash! I'm going to die tonight! Who will take care of my wife and daughters?' I clutched my seat and prayed with a fervor I've never felt before that I might live to see my girls grow up and to give my family the love and help they need."

With that, Ed paused for a second to gulp air and then slowly exhale to calm himself again. After a few seconds he continued, "Well, obviously we made it. We made an emergency landing in Indianapolis, and they got us all off the plane without anyone being

injured. Fifty paces or so from the plane, I fell on my knees and pro-
fusely thanked God in heaven for delivering us.

"They herded us into a special room in the Indianapolis airport,
and the first thing I did was find a phone and call my wife. I told her
what had happened and reassured her again and again that I was safe.
We cried together on the phone. I knew that other people in the
room could see and hear me, but I didn't care. Though I hadn't been
acting like it, I love my wife and children very much, and coming so
close to leaving them alone touched me as few other things in my life.

"You know what hit me later that night as I tried to sleep?" Ed
asked. "I realized that when it looked as if we would crash and die, I
didn't give a *single* thought to the president of my company or my
region's poor showing or whether I'd be unemployed the next day.
Not one of those things mattered. I'm a businessman—been one for
over twenty years—so let me say this in a businessman's language. In a
crippled plane somewhere over Indiana, I learned what the bottom
line in life is: It's the people I love and who love me—my family."

If you had been in that airplane, do you think you would have
come to the same conclusion as Ed?

Think about it just for a moment. If you faced a situation—a disease, a pending crash, a house ablaze—that created within you the
fear that you were about to die, what would your last thoughts be
about? Your job? Your bank account? Your prestige, fame, or notoriety?

Or your family?

When a cardiologist told Joe Beam several years ago that it
appeared he was in the middle of a heart attack, Joe suddenly found
himself strapped to a gurney being wheeled to an operating room for
an immediate heart catheterization. As his wife, Alice, walked beside
him holding his hand, Joe could think of only two things: First, his
thoughts went to his children, and he prayed that God would let him
live to help Alice raise them. Then, he thought of his wife, and he
pulled Alice near and softly said, "I'm so sorry for all the things I've
done to hurt you. Please forgive me for all the pain I've caused you.
And believe me when I tell you that I love you with all my heart."

Joe discovered the same thing Ed discovered. Next to his relation-ship with God, the "bottom line" of life is family.

Hopefully, you won't have to go through a harrowing, life-threatening situation like Ed and Joe experienced, but you *can* come to the same realization about your family that they finally reached about theirs: Your family is your most important responsibility, your most important achievement, and the most important legacy you'll leave when finally you depart this world. Your family is more important than your job, your income, your standard of living, or your ambitions.

God said this about a person and his or her family: "If anyone does not provide for his relatives, and especially for his immediate family, he has denied the faith and is worse than an unbeliever."[1]

While it is true that the immediate context of this verse is the material needs of one's family, it certainly isn't a stretch of the passage to infer that *any* of the needs of the family fall within its parameters—spiritual and emotional needs as well as physical needs. And this verse isn't only about caring for the family as a *whole*, but surely includes caring for the *individuals* who make up that family.

WHAT'S SO IMPORTANT ABOUT FAMILY?

That question can be answered with a biblical illustration. You may recall the Old Testament story of Esther, whom God positioned as queen so that she could save the people of Israel from utter and complete destruction. Esther's husband, King Xerxes, had been manipulated by the evil Haman to sign a decree that would effectively end the messianic line and prevent Jesus' coming centuries later. Whether or not Xerxes or Haman understood the consequences of annihilating the Jews, the Jewish people surely did. They knew that the Messiah had not yet come and that if their nation were destroyed, God's plan for sending a savior would be thwarted.

Of course, God was in control and would not allow that catastro-phe; that's why he placed Queen Esther, a Jewess, in the king's palace. To make sure she understood her responsibility, he told her through her cousin Mordecai, "If you remain silent at this time, relief and deliverance for the Jews will arise from another place, but you and your father's family will perish. And who knows but that you have come to royal position for such a time as this?"[2]

At first glance, this story may seem irrelevant to the importance of caring for one's family. But with reflection it's easy to see that this story has a moral that applies to today's fathers and mothers just as much as it applied to Esther so many centuries ago. Many forces are at work today, tearing families apart, destroying the basic unit of all civilization.

We must not let this happen. God calls upon us, like he called upon Esther, to take action to protect and nurture our families.

Throughout history, the state of the family has determined the state of individuals and nations. If you think that a grandiose statement, consider the pattern seen in the rise and fall of such great societies as ancient Egypt, Greece, and Rome. When those nations were at the peak of their power, glory, and prosperity, the family was highly valued and strong. But history makes it clear that when the quality of family life deteriorated, the strength of the nation deteriorated simultaneously.

The same holds true today. We are confronted daily with evidence that the quality of family life is crucial to our happiness, emotional well-being, and mental health. There isn't even a question about it any more: We know that poor relationships within the family are related to many of the problems in society.

A few years ago, in Little Rock, Arkansas, a social worker brought together the leaders of two gangs that had spread there from Los Angeles. You may have heard of them—the Crips and the Bloods. As these two angry young men sat on either side of a stage facing an audience of social workers, crime-victim advocates, and educators, they were peppered with questions about how their gangs operated and why they did what they did. Finally, in exasperation, someone in the audience sang out, "What would it take to put an end to you? To make your gangs go away...cease to exist?"

As a hush fell over the room, one of the gang members leaned into a microphone and uttered these startling words: "Hey, you get us a better fam'ly, and we won't need no gangs. My boys are all the fam'ly I got."

If what he said was true, then someone had seriously let this young man—and his compatriots—down. His mother? His father? Maybe even his brothers and sisters? We might even include his grandparents or uncles and aunts. Somewhere, somehow, those who should have been a family to this young man and all the other young, angry men in his gang had failed to be so.

And our nation is slowly decaying for it.

No, gangs are not our only problem—though their numbers are rising. Also feeding the decay is the fact that many today lack any kind of emotional connection with others. They have no emotional support from their current family, no ties to their past, and no tools for building a future. Young folks are starting families without ever having learned what a family should be. And to their new families they bring a host of emotional, spiritual, and material problems—all springing from the same root: the lack of strong families.

It's not just in the slums of Little Rock, Los Angeles, or Chicago that we see these problems. They're also in the posh suburbs of Atlanta, Omaha, and Palm Beach. They're in the smaller towns too—like Littleton, Colorado, and Paducah, Kentucky. And there are countless teens about to leave for college—who haven't joined gangs or shot anyone—who are empty and starved for the love of their families.

We have to stop this. And the only place to stop it is in our own families. That's where the battle must begin.

Esther expressed to her husband the same sentiment we should feel: "How can I bear to see disaster fall on my people? How can I bear to see the destruction of my family?"[3]

GOOD NEWS!

Don't despair. This isn't yet another book about how bad things are: This is a book of good news about how to make your family everything you want it to be! If you are as motivated as Esther to prevent your family's destruction and to prevent disaster from falling on our nation, this book can help.

How?

By showing you what it takes to make your family strong and healthy. You see, this book is based on more than twenty-five years of worldwide research. And this research has conclusively identified six characteristics that strong families have in common and has demonstrated the power of these "secrets" to give a family strength, happiness, and fulfillment. Think about it: Six secrets to family success *exist* and are being *successfully used* by families across this great planet. But these secrets are "open secrets" that anyone can know and use. These six characteristics are shared with you in this book so that you can embed them into your family!

A wonderfully diverse group of families contributed to the findings of this research: two-parent families, extended families, single-parent families, stepfamilies; families from all educational levels and from all economic levels; young families, middle-aged families, and older families; African-American, Asian-American, Native-American, Hispanic-American, and European-American families; families in North, Central, and South America; families in Western and Eastern Europe; families in South Africa and the South Pacific; families in the Middle East, East Asia, and Southeast Asia. They come from all walks of life, all faiths, all races—some rich and some poor. They come from every state in the nation and many countries around the world.

One of the fascinating aspects of this research is that it points to the possibility that the basic foundational qualities of emotionally healthy families—those underlying dynamics that contribute to family satisfaction and resilience—are remarkably similar from family to family and from culture to culture. Though it is undeniable that each family and each culture in the world is unique, mounting evidence leads to the proposition that healthy families around the world may be, in essence, more similar than different.

And through this book you have the unique opportunity to learn from strong families around the world as they share their secrets of success. They will teach us, not how families fail, but how families succeed.

This book, then, is a celebration of strong families and a sharing of the knowledge it takes to make your family strong. It is not based on opinion: It is based on twenty-five years of research with enough families from enough countries and backgrounds so that you can *know* what makes strong families. And as you would have thought, each of these six characteristics is right in the Bible.

And this is what we share with you.

WHAT IS A STRONG FAMILY?

Being a healthy family is more than being *without* problems; strong families have lots of problems—just like everyone else.

Before John DeFrain's grandmother, Effie DeFrain, died at age eighty-six, she lay in bed blind from cataracts, both legs amputated at the hip from complications of diabetes. Her middle-aged son, Orville, was noting the difficulties he was confronting in life at the time. She listened patiently. "Life," she responded without malice, "*is* troubles."

Strong families know about trouble. We could tell you about the Nebraska rancher and his family who have been forced to sell everything and start over because of financial losses. Or there's the Oklahoma family whose father is chronically ill. Or the young couple in Missouri who lost everything in a flood except each other and the cat.

To be a strong family is not to be without challenges. It is much, much more; it is the presence of guidelines for living and the ability to surmount life's inevitable challenges when they arise.

Strong families are pleasant, positive places to live because members have learned some beneficial ways of treating each other. Family members can count on each other for support, love, and loyalty. They can talk to each other; they enjoy each other.

Members of strong families feel good about themselves as a family unit or team; they have a sense of belonging with each other—a sense of *we*. At the same time, no individual gets lost or smothered; each family member is encouraged to develop his or her potential.

Strong families are able to survive the crises that come their way. They unite to meet challenges; they are effective problem solvers. They pull together to pull through. Perhaps good families can best be defined as places where we enter for comfort, development, and regeneration and places from which we go forth renewed and charged with power for positive living.

And what, by the way, is a family? Family, of course, includes parents and children, spouses, aunts, cousins, friends, and all those other folks we acquire by birth and by living. Any definition of family, then, needs to be broad and designed to be inclusive rather than exclusive. One definition we like is: A *family is two or more people who are committed to each other and who share intimacy, resources, decisions, and values.*

But this definition does not quite identify the quality that makes relationships in a family different from those in other areas of life—at work, for example. Some have suggested that it is unconditional love and knowing that family can be depended upon (commitment) that make a family different. Here's a simple way to express that distinguishing quality: A *good family is made up of people who love and care for each other always and regardless.*

Our research proves that families like these have six common characteristics. What are they? What are these six secrets of healthy, happy families? It's time to answer that question.

THE SIX QUALITIES OF STRONG FAMILIES

Six major qualities of strong families were uncovered in Nick Stinnett's original research in Oklahoma, and those same characteristics continued to emerge as the study expanded. In spite of cultural, political, and language differences, the strong families investigated around the world are very similar. Not only does this research consistently show these six characteristics; the findings are also validated by others who research families.[4]

Good families share six major qualities:

1. *Commitment*. Members of strong families are dedicated to promoting each other's welfare and happiness. They value the unity of the family.
2. *Appreciation and Affection*. Members of strong families show appreciation for each other a great deal. They can feel how good a family is.
3. *Positive Communication*. Members of good families have good communication skills and spend large amounts of time talking with each other.
4. *Time Together*. Strong families spend time—quality time in generous quantities—with each other.
5. *Spiritual Well-being*. Whether they go to formal religious services or not, strong families have a sense of a greater good or power in life. That belief gives them strength and purpose.
6. *The Ability to Cope with Stress and Crises*. Members of strong families are able to view stress or crises as opportunities to grow.

There they are. Six qualities that strong families have in common. It is all pretty simple, isn't it? Doesn't sound difficult at all, does it? And that's one of the difficulties we've discovered. The six steps to building strong families are so profoundly simple that they *can* be misleading! Why? Because simply *understanding* what we need to do to make our families work happily together is not enough. The principles of this book must be *lived out* in your family.

Strong families are made—step by step. People in strong families have to work at it, to nurture it. Constantly.

A POSSIBILITY AND AN INVITATION

Wouldn't it be nice if you could wave a magic wand and instantly create a good family environment? It would be very nice. But that's not how it works. Happy, strong families can, however, be built with time and effort.

"Impossible!" someone may protest. "My family has too many problems." If you think that, please change your thought process immediately. Experience has shown that if your family has problems—even *major* problems—the situation can be remedied and you can have a *fantastic* family life. You can do it by applying in your family the six steps found in this book.

Someone else may say, "I already have a good family life." Fantastic! But even for you we have a message, "It can be *better* and *stronger!*" If you lack in even one of the six areas—or if you can be stronger in any of the six areas—you can make your family even stronger and happier by using these six steps.

Even if you're only contemplating marriage, you can begin to ensure that your family will be strong and that your marriage will thrive to your golden wedding anniversary and beyond. These six steps are the key.

Each step has been repeatedly confirmed by the real experts—fourteen thousand strong families—and each is validated in the Book of books. If other families can do it, you can do it. No matter what your family is like right now.

This book is a guide to help you reach the happiness and strength you want in your family and in other interpersonal relationships. The strong families researched for this book are a beacon to light your way.

STEP ONE

COMMIT TO YOUR FAMILY

W hat can I do to make it right? How can we ever function as a family again? I've tried everything I know to do. I take Cindy out on a date at least once a week. We don't miss a counseling session with our therapist. I'm at every game the boys play and spend nearly every Saturday afternoon throwing the ball around the backyard with them. But it still doesn't seem right. It's like they can't forgive me completely. Like they're holding back somehow.

"Do I have to wait years for them to trust me again, or is there some magic wand you can wave to help me now?"

Joe Beam sat listening to Jeffrey, waiting patiently for a chance to respond to his continuing lamentation. Jeffrey was a wanderer returned to his family. Nearly nine months earlier, Jeffrey had left Cindy, his wife of twelve years, to move in with a woman he'd met in a chat room on the Internet. The romance started as a mindless flirtation but escalated in whirlwind fashion until it held so much power over Jeffrey that he was willing to sacrifice everything he held holy—including his family—to be immersed in the intoxication of his new love. The day he left his family, his two sons—ages six and nine—had shamelessly begged him not to go, not caring that the neighbors saw them crying and shouting at their father as they followed him to his

Blazer while he hauled yet another armload of clothes from his house. Jeffrey was so infatuated with his lover that he'd convinced himself that the boys would be better off without him. After all, he reasoned, children do better in a happy home than a troubled one.

It wasn't easy for Jeffrey to believe that lie as he tried to shut his sons' plaintive pleading from his consciousness.

But he did.

He left them standing there. As he slammed the car door and started his engine, he watched Cindy come from the house to wrap her arms around her sons and pull their faces to hers as she attempted to console them. Jeffrey didn't watch long. He couldn't. He gritted his teeth, shook the sight from his eyes, and rammed his car into reverse. Clearing his driveway, he turned the wheel hard, dropped the gearshift into drive, and floored the gas, screeching his tires as he fled his failure. He refused to look back at his wife or children as he drove out of their lives.

And into his dream.

It took only a few months to realize that his dream was actually a nightmare. The intoxication fizzled in the light of reality, and he found that his new love wasn't the woman he'd fantasized during their on-line romance.

Finally, in penitence and shame, he'd come to his senses and begged Cindy to take him back. She agreed, after much prayer and godly counsel, but insisted that as a condition of Jeffrey's return, they immediately enter intensive marriage therapy. Almost overnight, Jeffrey became a model husband and father. It was sixty days into his reunion with his family that he sat at the restaurant with Joe.

"So tell me, please. You're in the marriage and family business. Will my wife and children ever let me be as close to them as I once was? Are they gonna punish me the rest of my life?"

Joe leveled his gaze at Jeffrey and calmly replied, "They aren't punishing you. They're afraid of you."

"Afraid! Are you nuts? They've never had anything to fear from me. Even when I was totally crazy in sin, I never did anything that would harm Cindy or the boys or anybody else. Man, what're you talkin' about? They're not afraid of me!"

"Oh, yes they are." Joe continued. "But their fear isn't that you're going to hurt them *physically*. They're afraid that you're going to hurt them emotionally. You left once. What's keeping you from leaving again? That's what's happening under the surface for them. They're slightly withdrawn from you as a protection for themselves—just in case you leave them again."

Jeffrey sat in stunned silence for a few moments, turning the possibility over in his mind, and finally muttered, "But I thought they understood that by coming back I was proving that I'll never leave again. I figured that was just understood.

"I mean, it should be, shouldn't it?"

"Look, Jeffrey, whether it should or shouldn't be isn't the issue here. The issue is that your family will be unable to feel fully committed in their relationship with you until they are completely convinced of *your* total commitment to them. I have no doubt they want to be close and loving with you—just as you do—but you need to realize that any person, even your own child, finds it difficult to give unadulterated affection when he or she fears it won't be reciprocal. You came back, but you need to do more than just come back. You need to convince your wife and sons that from this day on you are committed to them until the day you die.

"You can't tell them too many times that you're committed. You can't do too much to prove it to them. As many times as it takes, you need to say to Cindy, to each boy, and sometimes to all three of them together, 'I'm here for good. Every day when I walk out that door, you can know that I'm coming back through it. I'm coming back when things are good. I'm coming back when things are bad. On happy days, sad days, frustrated days, or mad days. The only thing that can ever keep me from coming back through that door *every* day is for me to be dead. As long as I live, I'm committed to each one of you. No one and no thing will ever come between us again. This is the truth and always will be the truth from this moment on.'"

Jeffrey's eyes widened slightly as the awareness hit him. Cindy and his sons couldn't have the relationship with him that he and they wanted as long as they had to protect themselves in fear that he might leave again. He realized that the flaw wasn't in them and that he shouldn't feel anger or resentment toward them for being afraid; he'd created this scenario, and only he could fix it.

The good news is that he did fix it. It took awhile, but armed with awareness and determination, he rebuilt his family's happiness by starting at the right place. He rebuilt it by laying well and true the foundation of *commitment*.

THE FOUNDATION FIRM

In a 1994 meeting with Nick Stinnett, Joe pressed, "C'mon, Nick. I know you say that all six characteristics are important for family strength, but I'm a trainer by trade, and trainers always want to know where to start. If I could only help a couple learn to do *one* thing, which of the six would it be? What's the most important secret for having a strong family?"

Nick smiled in reply, "Joe, you *know* how reluctant I am to pinpoint just one characteristic, because *all* six are of such vital importance. But since you keep asking, I will tell you. There is one that we consider to be the foundation on which the other five are built.

"It's commitment."

Nick went on to explain that the dictionary might describe commitment as a pledge or obligation. In his research he'd discovered that strong families understand commitment to mean that the family comes first. He's heard strong families say this in many ways:

My *wife and kids are the most important part of my life.*

I'm *convincing my husband that we should take the children and fly back East to visit his father for Thanksgiving. I know it's expensive and this is a busy work time for us, but Pop is eighty-three years old, and I want the children to know their grandfather. That's what family is all about.*

I look forward to growing old with my wife. Sometimes I can visualize us sitting on the front porch together in our retirement, holding hands, rocking in unison, and benignly gossiping about our neighbors as we wave to them on the sidewalk.

The research conducted by Drs. Stinnett and DeFrain shows that commitment is the bedrock on which every family must be built. When each family member knows that the others are there and always will be there and that the family is above everything else—work, recreation, other people, crises, or whatever—that family has the ability to develop the other five characteristics that make them strong and happy. No one in a committed family lives in fear that he or she might be booted out or that some other family member will abandon them. In the atmosphere of trust and security that mutual commitment creates, every family member can survive any bad time or personal failure. They aren't afraid to expose their emotions and vulnerabilities. Neither are they afraid to love and forgive the idiosyncrasies or failures of each other.

SIX CHARACTERISTICS OF COMMITMENT

Commitment creates the warm, loving, accepting environment in which families grow. It offers a harbor that shelters family members from the destructive forces of fear, anxiety, rejection, and loneliness.

It's no wonder that commitment serves as the basis for everything else. When family members are committed to the family unit and to each of the individuals in the family, the other key characteristics can be built on that foundation.

What, then, does it mean to be committed? Six characteristics of commitment exist in strong marriages.

CHARACTERISTIC #1—COMMITMENT TO MARRIAGE

At the heart of commitment to the family unit is dedication to the marriage relationship. When both husband and wife fulfill their commitment to each other, they set the stage for all other commitments a family should have.

Kathy Simon highlighted this fact when she conducted a study focusing on "great fathers" in their middle years—experienced dads who felt they were doing a fine job rearing their kids.[1] Nearly four hundred fathers from across the United States participated in Kathy's research, and in her study she made a number of remarkable findings. One of her discoveries underscores our discussion here.

Kathy came to John DeFrain as she was finishing her research and asked, "Do you know what the greatest gift a father can give his children is?" With thousands of cumulative years of experience to back them up, the fathers she studied had shared all kinds of good advice, but one gift was mentioned more frequently than any other.

"What is it, John? What did these fathers repeatedly say was the greatest gift?" Kathy asked with a mischievous twinkle in her eye.

In spite of her obviously pending ambush, John took the bait. "I *am* a trained professional," he thought to himself. "I *can* figure this out!"

As the imaginary contest clock ticked off the seconds, he mentally ran through the possibilities and finally blurted out with confidence, "The greatest gift fathers give their children is their time, their love, and their energy so that the children develop optimal self-esteem!"

"Buzzzzzzzz! Wrong!" Kathy laughed. "The greatest gift a father can give his children is a happy marriage."

Many of the men in Kathy's study had experienced a divorce and had seen the pain that marital discord and dissolution caused their children. But whether or not they had been through divorce, the fathers recognized that their children's well-being was intimately related to the strength of their parents' marriage. If the marriage was going poorly, to a great degree, so went the lives of the children.

If you're a single parent, please don't be dismayed or discouraged at these words. Countless single parents are doing a great job and are to be applauded for their extraordinary efforts to nurture their kids. When families are torn by anger, violence, sexual abuse, alcohol, drug-related difficulties, and many other sin-induced problems, divorce sometimes happens. For some, divorce is a safety valve, a last-ditch effort to end the physical and emotional abuse for everyone, including the children. If that describes you, don't despair. This book is about how to have a happy and strong family no matter what your family unit is like right now.

With that said, let us return again to our point: Families founded upon a strong marriage can be truly wonderful places in which to live, as the fathers in Kathy's study pointed out.

Some parents focus so much on rearing the children, paying the bills, and keeping the car running that they forget the importance of their marriage. As a result, the marriage degenerates and can even fail. This is a grave mistake. Children do best in homes with happy parents who love each other and demonstrate that love in everyday commitment.

Kids who see their parents loving each other feel secure in the longevity of the family. There is a sense in which their parents' commitment to each other also shows the parents' commitment to the children and to the family as a whole.

The Commandment of God

God sees the commitment of husband and wife to each other as so crucial to families that he robustly condemned any violation of that marital commitment. In the Old Testament, he said that to violate the marriage covenant is to "break faith" (NIV) or "deal treacherously" (KJV, NKJV, ASV) with one's spouse. With those words, he makes it clear that marriage is a covenant between husband and wife and that breaking or ending that covenant is to sin—not just against the mate, but against God himself. Look at how he words it in the book of Malachi:

> Another thing you do: You flood the LORD'S altar with tears. You weep and wail because he no longer pays attention to your offerings or accepts them with pleasure from your hands. You ask, "Why?" It is because the LORD is acting as the witness between you and the wife of your youth, because you have broken faith with her, though she is your partner, the wife of your marriage covenant.

Has not the LORD made them one? In flesh and spirit they are his. And why one? Because he was seeking godly offspring. So guard yourself in your spirit, and do not break faith with the wife of your youth.

"I hate divorce," says the LORD God of Israel, "and I hate a man's covering himself with violence as well as with his garment," says the LORD Almighty.

So guard yourself in your spirit, and do not break faith.[2]

In the New Testament, Jesus made it clear that if it weren't for the hardness of the hearts of humans, divorce wouldn't exist at all.[3] God never wanted it, and humankind shouldn't want it either.

But the goal here isn't just to stay married; it is to be committed to making the marriage all that it can be. God commands that a husband love his wife as Christ loves the church[4] and that he love her as his own body.[5] He even went so far as to make the thought-provoking statement, "He who loves his wife loves himself."[6] God also commands wives to love their husbands and children.[7]

The commitment to be there and not abandon each other, no matter what, is the foundation. But the commitment goes further. It says, "We will do whatever it takes to love each other as we should."[8]

Marriage Commitment Includes Sexual Fidelity

After years of comprehensive sex research, the world's most prominent sex researchers, William Masters and Virginia Johnson, concluded that one of the most important factors contributing to satisfaction in a sexual relationship is the presence of commitment.[9] Strong families have known this all along. Read what a few of them have said on the subject:

I know it seems like everybody is having affairs—if you can believe gossip—but we are old-fashioned and faithful. I can only imagine bad things from an affair: hurt, deceit, family break-up. Being true to each other reinforces our bond.

Being faithful to each other sexually is just a part of being honest with each other.

For us, sexual faithfulness is essential. There is a security, a special feeling of knowing you are the only one with whom your spouse chooses to have sex. I think most people—no matter what they say—can't handle affairs. When one partner has an affair, it does bad things to the self-esteem of the other. An affair sends too many devastating messages: "You are not special; you are replaceable" or, "You are not satisfying me sexually."

The husbands or wives who wrote those comments believe strongly in the sanctity of marriage and hold themselves to a commitment of sexual fidelity. That standard is not only wise; it is biblical. Under the Old Testament law, those who committed adultery were executed.[10] The New Testament has this to say: "Marriage should be honored by all, and the marriage bed kept pure, for God will judge the adulterer and all the sexually immoral."[11]

But does all of this mean that if a marriage has suffered infidelity it cannot ever be strong again?

If the Promise Is Broken

Commitment and sexual fidelity are so closely linked in most people's minds that an extramarital sexual affair is regarded as the ultimate threat to a marriage. No other enemy seems as dangerous as the "other" man or woman. No hurt seems as deep as betrayal by a husband or wife.

Because an extramarital affair poses such a potent threat, it is important that we briefly consider the extent of extramarital sex, the dynamics involved, and more importantly, how strong families deal with such issues.

It's difficult to say with certainty how widespread extramarital sex is in this country. For obvious reasons, the Census Bureau has not added a question about it on its ever-expanding questionnaire. Furthermore, the dynamics of affairs are difficult to sort out. Each affair is unique. For example, some married people become involved with a stranger; others with a friend—maybe even a person who is a best friend to the couple or spouse. Some strayers have only one affair;

others are chronic philanderers. Extramarital liaisons differ in duration too—from one-night stands to long-term relationships.[12]

One wife we interviewed was aware of the complexities.

I don't know what I'd do if Chuck had a fling with someone else. I guess it would depend on lots of things. If he got drunk at a convention and had a one-night romance, it would be easier to accept than if I found out he'd had a three-year affair with his secretary. Although both involve sex outside of marriage and both would crush my heart, they don't seem exactly the same.

While few spouses are as analytical as the wife quoted above, her statement corresponds to what appears to be an instinctive awareness within hurt spouses. There is a difference in the kind of hurt felt by those whose spouses were involved in relationship affairs and the kind of hurt felt by those whose spouses were involved in short-lived affairs. Either affair creates tremendous hurt, but greater damage was almost always experienced by those whose spouses had longer, more-involved relationship affairs.

Another dynamic also comes into play. While any adultery is devastating, repeated instances of adultery are so ruinous that they create a scenario where it's almost impossible to salvage the marriage. In contrast, one-time affairs typically can be overcome if each partner is willing to do the work to get past the affair.[13]

Obviously, for one's spiritual, emotional, familial, and marital health, extramarital involvements should be avoided at all cost. Commitment to God and to marriage can serve as the fortress that prevents straying.

But what if it does happen? What then?

The End or a New Beginning

More than a few strong families have dealt with extramarital sexual issues. Remember, strong families are not more pure than other families; they have problems too. And sometimes, strong families have to face infidelity. But it's how strong families deal with their problems—including adultery—that distinguishes them from other families. It may surprise you to know that for some couples who now have strong marriages, overcoming an infidelity crisis in their marriage was an important step in their long process of becoming strong. This is certainly not an endorsement of extramarital sex as a way of improving marriage. And none of the strong families in this study recommended anything but sexual exclusivity. On the other hand, an extramarital involvement need not automatically end a marriage. Couples who are committed to each other can overcome such an evil. As they work through the hurt and pain, they can even use the sin as a catalyst for growth in a marriage.

Doubt that?

Consider the following.

Anne and Lionel's Story

Snow fell quietly in South Dakota on that bitter cold January night, but Anne noticed neither the temperature nor the beauty of the blanketed landscape. Newscasters opened their 10 P.M. broadcast with unnerving good cheer, causing Anne to mute her TV before padding quietly into her bathroom. In no hurry, she opened the closet door and almost casually searched through a jumbled basket of unused vitamins and discarded medicine for the sleeping pills she knew were there. It took less than a minute to find them. Drifting mindlessly back to her bedroom, she methodically retrieved from her dresser a tumbler filled with vodka. She stared at it for a moment, as if confused about where it came from, and then she continued to her bed with no apparent concern that she was carrying her death in her left hand and the nectar to wash it down in her right.

She hesitated only slightly before beginning to swallow them—first one, then three or four together—until the bottle was empty. The undiluted vodka should have burned her throat as she sloshed in enough to get each batch of pills down, but she seemed to be past feeling. When she was done, she lay on her bed, arranged the covers just so, and waited without emotion for the welcome oblivion.

Why did Anne do such a thing? Why would anyone take such a deluded path in search of peace? We'll let her husband, Lionel, explain.

Several months prior to that night, I became involved with Sandy. She works with me.

Before you judge me, at least understand that I didn't mean for it to happen. It started with innocent conversations that came during short breaks in long hours working together. I seemed drawn to her, and the more I got to know her, the more attractive she became to me. I realized I was sexually interested in her when out of the blue I began to fantasize about seducing her. I felt a little guilty thinking things like that, but it seemed so innocent, and I reassured myself that it wouldn't ever lead to anything. Then one day I kidded her about how many men she thought had fantasized about her.

That was a mistake.

She reacted with some suggestive comments of her own. Low-key, of course, but sexy just the same. It didn't take long for me to realize that she was attracted to me just like I was to her. We played around with that kind of talk for several days, which made for some stimulating sexual tension between us. We made sort of a running game out of it.

Guess I should've run from what was starting to happen, but I really enjoyed talking with her, and I liked the developing relationship—not just the sexual innuendoes, you understand, but everything about her. Well, whatever we had going picked up steam, and we started finding many reasons to be together. And then one day—it seems like a dream now—we wound up slipping off together and making love.

I'll never forget how that felt. One minute I was drunk on ecstasy, and the next, when it hit me what I had just done, I was filled with complete and total humiliation. I wanted God to strike me dead right on the spot. Kinda thought he might too. I prayed and cried and begged for mercy. If you had asked me then if I would ever commit adultery again, I would've told you that it could never happen again, that I could never face that kind of guilt and shame—ever.

I think it was two weeks before we sneaked off again. Just as soon as the guilt subsided, I started remembering the pleasure, the excitement. Just being alone with Sandy was unbelievable.

It didn't happen overnight, but within a few weeks we were meeting regularly. I felt as if I were in love for the first time in my life. And the crazy thing is that I still loved Anne. Just in a different way than how I loved Sandy.

I never felt that I became involved with Sandy because of any deficit in my marriage. All along I would have told you that I loved my wife very much and that our relationship—including sex—was great.

I think, for me, the whole reason for getting involved in the affair had something to do with my male ego and desires I didn't know I had. It was mighty flattering to know that a woman found me attractive and wanted me. Sandy always made elaborate preparations for our "dates"—special meals or wine, candles, soft music. And she always was so erotic and seductive.

Our affair lasted for several months, and we thought we were keeping it secret. Actually, people at the office figured it out early on. I mean, how could they not? Both of us disappearing at the same time for a couple hours. When I realized that they knew, I panicked and became afraid that Anne would find out through gossip.

So I told her.

It turned out, she had suspicions about what was going on, though she didn't want to believe it until I confessed it to her. She knows me better than anyone. I tried to console Anne by telling her that I still loved her but that I loved Sandy in a different way. Like a fool, I tried to convince her it wasn't bad for a man to love two women. One day I even brought home some books that said an affair could be a good way to expand a network of loving relationships.

You can imagine how that went over. She didn't subscribe to that idiocy, and I don't guess I truly did, but it was a good rationalization. Anne said she was leaving me, but I convinced her to stay by telling her I'd stop the affair immediately. I even started going to church with her again. But I didn't stop, and it didn't take long for Anne to sense it. As soon as she allowed herself to believe I was involved with Sandy again, Anne contacted a lawyer.

When it finally hit me that she really was going to divorce me, I fell apart. I couldn't take the thought of losing her. I hadn't wanted to hurt

Anne, as stupid as that may sound, and I didn't want our relationship destroyed. What I had with Sandy just didn't compensate.

I spent a sleepless night in soul searching. The next day I met Sandy for dinner and told her it was over. It wasn't easy to walk away from what I had with her. But I was relieved, too, you know? Deep within me, I knew I was doing the right thing. I'd pretty well quit thinking about God sometime back after I lost my fear of him punishing me, but when I left Sandy that night, I sort of felt like God was smiling at me, saying something like, "Welcome back, Lionel."

I couldn't wait to get home and convince Anne that it really was over, that I would do anything if she could only forgive me and not leave me. When I let myself in, the house was much too quiet. As I reached the bedroom door, the scene before me was like a surreal dream. By the flickering light of the silent TV, I could see Anne, tucked in bed so nice and neat, and on the nightstand next to our bed was an empty bottle of sleeping pills. I ran to her and froze when I reached the bed. She had no expression on her face. None. She just lay there with her eyes closed, breathing long, uneven breaths that were several seconds apart.

I can't tell you how long it took the paramedics to get there, but it seemed like forever. I kneeled beside her, holding her hands in mine, and begged God not to let her die for what I had done. I didn't sense his smiling now. I couldn't focus on him at all. All I could do was watch Anne's chest rise sporadically as she drew another breath and beg God over and over to spare her.

She lived. And she forgave me. I brought her home from the hospital, and we immediately started the tough process of rebuilding our marriage. I requested and received a job reassignment where I wouldn't have any contact with Sandy. And I began to court Anne again. We'd meet a couple times a week for lunch, and I always brought flowers or a gift. We also had "dates" at least one or two nights a week during which we worked out a lot of the hurt and bad feelings. I must've told Anne a thousand times that I love her and that I will always be there for her from now on, no matter what.

It took nearly a year, but we finally got to the point where we felt we needed to renew our marriage vows. We did it on our anniversary. We invited a few close friends to a beautiful little chapel and got married all over again.

Our marriage is closer and stronger than before. We've survived the worst that can happen to us, and we're together for life.

As you read the story of Anne and Lionel, you may have thought, "Why tell us so much about how it happened and how bad it became?" The reason is simple. It's important that you see how a loving husband (or wife, for that matter) can become so enamored with another person that he could cheat on his wife. No, there's no justification. Adultery is a terrible thing and never has any just cause for happening. But we all need to realize how destructive it is to the spouse who is sinned against. Anne, though absolutely wrong in her effort to kill herself, suffered terribly as a result of her husband's adultery.

But even in a case so bad that it nearly causes the death of a spouse, there can be healing and hope. When both parties in a marriage decide to commit themselves to each other with a commitment that surpasses their attraction or attention to any other person or thing, they can develop a healthy, loving marriage and a healthy, loving family. Even if the commitment in a relationship has been violated, it can be restored, and when it is, the relationship can heal and become strong!

CHARACTERISTIC #2—COMMITMENT TO EACH INDIVIDUAL

Commitment isn't only to the family as a unit or between husband and wife; in strong families, it is also to each individual in the family. As one Florida mother commented,

Each person forms a part of the family, and each part is precious.

This kind of commitment helps everyone in the family feel worthwhile and secure. An Illinois wife provides insight into this:

About ten years ago, after a brief physical illness and a change of jobs, something happened to me—to my mind and my emotions. I guess I became mentally sick. I lost control of my life and became so depressed that I could not function. Needless to say, I was not enjoyable to be around.

Probably no one will ever know all of the causes for that bad period in my life, but I can tell you that my family didn't give up on me. My husband searched until he found an excellent team of physicians to treat my medical problems. With their help, he located a counselor for me. He had to do all this for me, because a depressed person has no energy or initiative.

My daughter rearranged her schedule in order to drive me the forty miles to Springfield for my weekly counseling sessions. She always planned something special for our trips to the city—some shopping, a nice lunch, or a museum—that would boost my spirit.

My sister came by the house two or three times a week. She'd say she came for coffee or to talk, but she'd manage to tidy up the kitchen, do some laundry, weed a flower bed, or vacuum while she was there.

After a few weeks of the deepest depression, I began to feel a bit better. My complete recovery took nearly a year.

I am eternally grateful to a few close friends and to my church for helping in my recovery. But most especially, I am grateful to my family. As sick as I was, I was always aware of their support and patience.

Members of strong families express their commitment to one another—not just in words, but through investments of time and energy. Their commitment is active and obvious.

The story of another strong family illustrates this. Mary and Rob have been married for twenty-eight years and have three children. Their middle child, Erin, now twenty-four, is mentally retarded. From the time she was born, they united as a family to help Erin become all she could be, just as they did for each other family member. Mary devoted countless hours to an intensive home-therapy program when Erin was young. Older brother Kit and his wife include Erin in their vacation each year and plan special activities of interest to her. Younger sister Judy helped Erin find a job and worked with her until she could handle it alone. The entire family has been active in advocacy for persons with special needs. Mary speaks of their commitment to each other when she says,

> *We are a team; family is the heart and center of our thoughts. We pitch in to help because if one of us is in pain, we all hurt. Each of us is important, sort of like the Three Musketeers—"one for all and all for one!"*

This concept of commitment is as valid today as it was in Bible times. In the early church it was understood that families took care of each member—even widowed mothers or aunts—so that the church could concentrate on helping those who had no family.[14] Strong families take care of their own. Each and every one.

Giving Each Other 100 Percent

Knowing that everyone in the family is committed to one another helps each person feel a sense of belonging. One young woman described it this way:

> *I grew up in a rotten family, so I think I know a little about them. As nearly as I can describe it, a troubled family is like a sieve. People drain in; people drain out. If you drain out, it doesn't matter much to anyone.*
>
> *I'm in a happy family now. My husband and his folks are wonderful people. It wasn't easy to get into the family. Strong families are closed. Not unfriendly, but you can immediately feel the love and the caring for each other, and they aren't going to throw that away for any outsider who stumbles in. Of course, I know they won't let me go away easily either. I belong.*

An Oklahoma man comments on this total involvement in each other's lives:

> *I like to think of it as being 100 percent for each other. And an incident from my childhood demonstrates this kind of commitment. I was four*

years old, and we lived on a farm in Alabama. The house was set on a hill several yards from a busy highway. One summer morning my mother told me she was going to walk down to the mailbox, which was located just across the highway, to get the mail. She asked if I wanted to go. I was busy playing and told her no very emphatically. I watched her walk down the hill. As she approached the mailbox, I changed my mind about going. I began to run very fast. As I ran I yelled, "I'm coming! I'm coming!" What flashed through her mind must have been terror as she turned to see me nearing the highway. For she also saw a car—to which I was oblivious—coming at high speed. She knew in that instant that I wouldn't stop and the car wouldn't stop and I would surely be killed. She dropped the mail, raced across the path of the speeding car and scooped me up. We both fell on the shoulder of the highway. The car—which never slowed—barely missed us. My mother narrowly escaped death saving my life.

I've often thought about that incident in years since. It was one of my favorite stories as a child; I loved to hear it told and retold. As I got older, we joked about Mom moving so fast. But as you might guess, even in times when I strongly disagree with my mother or become irritated by something she does, I never doubt her 100 percent commitment to me.

Shared Goals

The involvement of strong family members in each other's lives is also reflected in the goals they share. Common goals encourage commitment by giving direction and purpose to the family. Each person has a part and fits somewhere in the fulfillment of the family goals. Not only is each family member taken care of; he or she also enjoys the satisfaction of contributing to the family as a whole.

Sometimes family strength is a goal; other times the family pursues a specific goal together.

A good, happy, successful—whatever you want to call it—family is important to us. Whenever we get sidetracked from that, we remind ourselves and get back on track.

Our goals as a family include working this business and having fun together when the work is finished.

We pull together on many projects. Right now we're training our new puppy and doing some renovation of the backyard.

CHARACTERISTIC #3—COMMITMENT TO PUTTING FIRST THINGS FIRST

Although circumstances as intense as an extramarital sexual affair or the emotional breakdown of a family member obviously pose powerful threats to family solidarity, many families have found their commitment to each other eroded by a less obvious enemy: misplaced priorities. Things that appear important gradually move themselves to the head of the line, demanding more focus than the family itself. Strong families realize that the family comes first and don't allow other aspects of life—no matter how important they may seem—to dilute their commitment.

When Work Gets in the Way

Work and the demands of work—time, attention, energy—all too often infringe on family. When a person is more committed to work than to family, it's almost as if that person is having an affair against the whole family. In extramarital affairs, the primary person hurt is the spouse. In work affairs, everyone suffers.

What do strong families do about the pressures of work on family life? Obviously, they don't quit working altogether.[15] One thing they do is continually remind themselves that family is more important than income, career, or prestige. Perhaps we could slightly alter a quote from Jesus of Nazareth to get the proper perspective about the relative importance of income or career in relation to one's family. He said, "What good will it be for a man if he gains the whole world, yet forfeits his soul? Or what can a man give in exchange for his soul?"[16] Of course, the answer lies in the rhetorical question. Nothing justifies losing one's soul. Now, change his words just slightly and see another truth that's just as valid: "What good will it be for you to become rich or famous, yet forfeit your family? What amount of money or what level of career advancement will you pursue in exchange for your family?"

No earthly goal or pursuit justifies losing one's family.

A businessman from a strong family tells about his experience:

Flashes of insight take only an instant, and I'm thankful for one I had on an airplane one afternoon. I was off on my usual business travel, which took me away from home three or four days a week. I'd left a teenager disappointed because I would miss her dance recital. My wife felt so swamped that she'd described herself as a de facto single parent. I had a growing sense of alienation from my family; sometimes I missed chunks of their lives.

Indignantly I thought, "Yeah, but they don't mind the money I make. I have work to do. It's important!" Then the flash of insight came.

What frontier was I crossing? I wasn't curing cancer or bringing world peace. My company markets a soft drink. A soft drink! Granted, we sell it all over Ohio and are moving into the Pittsburgh market, but how many gallons of soft drink would I be willing to trade for my family?

I didn't quit. I enjoy sales, and it's a good job. I make good money. But I did learn to say no to some company demands. And now I plan my travel so that I have more time at home. Sometimes I take my wife or daughter along.

In a few years I'll retire, and within a few months of that, I'll be forgotten in the soft drink market.

But I'll still be a husband and father. I'll be that until I die.

Sometimes it takes courage to affirm the valuable things in life, as one wife explains:

We were on a merry-go-round: There was no time for anything but work, we never seemed to have enough money, and we were continually juggling schedules and dollars. Something had to give. It was scary, but I quit my job so we'd have more time for family.

The surprising thing is: Now we have more money as well. Because I have time to cook, we don't eat out as often; I can feed us nutritiously at home for half of what it costs to eat out. I shop garage sales and thrift stores for the kids' clothes and household stuff. We sold our second car, which saved money on gas, maintenance, tags, and insurance. All in all, we ended up with about fifteen dollars more each week than before, but now we feel sane. When the kids are older, I may work again.

Right now, I am content to help them grow up, to continue my church involvement, and to make contributions in ways other than a salary.

Other families shared similar stories:

I could have the boat I want if I were willing to take a second job on weekends. Only problem is, I'd have no time to go fishing, so I wouldn't need the boat!

We could have more things—a fancy car, new furniture, bigger house—if I worked outside the home. But we value our time together. Besides, someone needs to be there as a center for our family. Right now, that's my most important task.

But what happens when both spouses work and neither can quit? Some strong families manage the pressures of work by balancing work and home. Many couples do that by sharing responsibilities for child-rearing and housework more equally. Sometimes the changes are not smooth, as one mother of two explained:

Bills were piling up. We had to choose between taking our kids out of a great private school or my going to work. We prayed about it, thought about home schooling, and finally decided that the kids needed what they would learn in the local Christian school. I found a job that paid enough to make that happen, but my working outside the home required more of an adjustment for my family than we'd expected.

Bill hated it. I didn't have time to dote on him anymore. And the kids hated it. Teddy cried in school because I was gone a lot. And David acted out at home to get my attention. For a while it looked as if all the good that would come from the excellent education would be lost because of my family's negative reaction to my not being at home for the first time in my married life. But we'd prayed about the decision and still felt it was the right one, even if things weren't yet going as we'd expected.

Over the next few months, things got worse—a lot worse. For the first time in our married life, the word divorce came up, and we were both scared.

So we've been talking. A lot. And things are changing—slowly but steadily. Bill is slowing down in his work; he sees it isn't all that important to climb the corporate ladder. By the time he got enough promotions for me to quit work, the boys would be out of school anyway. Bill does his job well and still brings home the same paycheck, but he isn't at work all the time anymore. He takes more time with the kids and with me. And I have learned from his mistakes, so I am not going to be smothered by my new career either. I may continue to work after the boys finish school, just to feel I'm contributing something to society, but I won't let my job now or later ever cause my family to come second—not when my children are at home and not after they grow up and move on.

The boys help with the dishes and cook and vacuum. They gripe, but they are proud of their new skills, and they earn allowances.

All in all, we've adjusted well, and the boys are doing great in school. Just the other night, my oldest son was explaining the intricacies of a passage in Acts they had been discussing in their Bible class at school. I could almost see him being a Bible professor some day.

We have changed. Growth hurts—it always does. But it is good.

Many of the women in the strong families studied have wrestled with combining career and family. What are some of their secrets for survival?

I learned I could not be everything to everyone. No Superwoman outfits for me! I had to decide what was important and let other things go. For example, I have reduced community activities. It would be unrealistic to try to do volunteer work on top of everything else.

I have always operated on the idea that there is a point of diminishing returns. By that I mean a point when more hours on the job don't yield that much. If I get tired of my job or work myself into a state of nervous exhaustion, I'm not much help to anyone. I don't put in overtime unless it can't be avoided. I need to go home to refresh myself and enjoy being with my family.

I think of myself as having ten energy units per day, and I budget their expenditure. Work would eat up nine and a half if I let it. Instead, I plan five energy units for work, three for the children, two for me and John. During rush times, I may have to adjust to eight for work, two at home. But by being aware of my budget, I can always save some units for home.

It helps to have a supportive spouse and children who are responsible [about chores] and responsive to my needs.

When I got my first job, my initial reaction was, "How can I work with three children?" I was concerned for their care, so I located a good home daycare provider and paid her twice the going rate. I wanted her to feel responsible for the children.

When I can afford it, I hire someone to do the housework. We use paper plates for snacks. The children have chores; we use a chart to keep track of who does what. Some things just don't get done.

Whether one or both spouses work outside the home, commitment means a promise by both spouses to make the marriage and the family operate as they should. Both husbands and wives in strong families are willing to change and lend a helping hand to the other. The support and aid they give to each other (and to their children) are visible manifestations of their commitment to each other and to the family. A few of their comments illustrate this:

My husband's business is seasonal, so some periods are quite hectic for him. I try to help by mowing the lawn and doing some of the other things he normally does around the house.

My husband helps me with the kids and around the house without having to be asked.

We were not able to make it financially any longer on the farm. So we sold everything and moved to town. My wife is teaching school to support us while I go back to the university to train for another career.

When Life Gets Hectic

When asked, "How do you cope with work, family, and all your other activities?" one mother responded by laughing, "Not very well!" All of us feel that way at times, and not just about work issues. The press to do many things seems to be part of modern life. Besides work, there's recreation, community activities, PTA, church, Scouts, sports leagues, clubs, volunteer work, and on the list could go.

How do we manage the busy pace of life without hurting our families? Our strong families give us the answer. Their lives get hectic and fragmented too. But they control the madness. One husband told us:

Things can creep up on you. No one would take on so many involvements all at once. But over the years, I had joined a fraternal organization, volunteered to help with my son's soccer team, begun teaching a class at church, enrolled in a class to learn how to do my own income tax returns, and begun swimming each day at the YMCA. This is all in addition to work, yard, and car care. It was too much. One week I had only one night at home. I decided that I could hire someone to do the income tax, attend every other fraternal meeting, and swim four days a week. If that doesn't help as much as I need, I'll let the soccer team win without me.

Priority-Setting Sessions

Numerous families described a family priority-setting session. Some families convened once a week, some once a month, and others biannually. Some write down their lists; others do the exercise mentally. The general principle was described by a Nebraska mother:

We have a family council about once a month to review our situation. We discuss who's doing what, accomplishments, new goals, et cetera. An ongoing problem is that of too little time and too much to do. We've found the best way to reduce the stress is to evaluate our involvements and eliminate some. This usually isn't hard. And it's a good learning experience for the children in deciding what satisfies them the most and what they want to focus attention on. Brian, for example, has decided that he likes soccer better than Scouts. Matt opted to try karate lessons this fall instead of flag football. We knew that doing both was out of the question.

I have been taking evening classes at the community college, but I decided to put those on hold this semester. We have some major remodeling projects planned that I will need to attend to.

We always finish family council feeling less tense and harried than before.

Ending Fragmentation

When fragmentation is the issue, each family member signifies his or her individual commitment by cutting outside activities so that family takes precedence. Andy and Patricia provide another example of how strong families go on the offensive. They are a young couple beset by pressures: job, mortgage, car payments, church work, in-laws—the whole kettle of fish. They were so strung out by extraneous matters that there was no time for love. There was time to fix the transmission, time for the church ice-cream social, but there was no time for love.

So they sat down with their calendars and planned that time for the next six months. Here are their rules:

- ◆ One night meeting a week (No more!)
- ◆ No more than forty hours on the job a week
- ◆ No work can be brought home
- ◆ One date per week at least four hours in length (Yes, a date! Just like in high school; only fun!)
- ◆ One hour of genuine talking per day—not per week, like so many people do, but per day
- ◆ At the end of six months, plan for the next six

Sometimes Priority Means Sacrifice

Athletes forego dessert, cigarettes, coffee, and late nights to get into top physical condition. Musicians and artists discipline themselves to invest the necessary time to refine their skills, and they have to sacrifice other things in order to do this.

The strong families who mentioned cutting out activities, civic involvements, or work demands in order to enhance family life realize that it isn't enough to give family their leftover time. Leftover time isn't enough to produce successful musicians or athletes. Why expect it to be enough to produce a successful family?

We usually think about sacrifice as giving up something really important. However, this is often not the case. Sometimes we discover, as the strong families explained, that we don't even miss the things we abandon in order to make a larger investment in our families.

One man interviewed in Denver, for example, quit a new job for the sake of his family. A few months earlier, he had left a longtime career in education to become an administrative assistant to a hotel financier.

His new job turned out to be fast-paced and all-consuming. Sure, there was plenty of money, prestige, and flash, but there were also many evening meetings, extended travel, and extra hours.

The boss told me that if I worked hard like this for five years, I would be a millionaire. That may have been the case, but in a few months time, I concluded that I'd more likely be divorced or dead. I didn't like what I was doing. The long hours were killing me, and I missed my family.

The boss was perfectly happy seeing his wife and children between 8:00 and 10:00 P.M. three nights a week. He thought that was about right for any husband.

I'm going to get back into education. I suppose a lot of people would think me stupid to give up money and power for my family. But the way I look at it, I was giving up more by sacrificing my family. I don't regret my decision a bit.

At the heart of sacrifice is the ability to put the best interests of someone else ahead of self—an unselfish attitude. This unselfishness is apparent in the comments of strong families.

Sometimes sacrifices have to be made. One time I may give up something for the benefit of my wife or child. At other times they give up something for me. No one feels martyred by this; it's a give-and-take process.

I was both amused and pleased by a conversation between my boys yesterday at the zoo. The zoo has recorded informational messages at each exhibit that are activated by a special zoo key for children. The boys immediately put up a clamor to have the key. They enjoyed the recordings, but as we headed for the exit to go home, the question of who would keep the key arose. Each said, "I want it." Then Dan, the ten-year-old, said, "You can keep it in your room." And Chris, who's eight, responded, "No, you keep it. We can share." It was clear that although each boy wanted the key, neither wanted to hurt a brother. The desire to be nice to one another was greater than the urge to satisfy self.

CHARACTERISTIC #4—COMMITMENT TO HONESTY

Honesty is an important measure of commitment in a family. When people recite the strengths of their families, it is remarkable how often honesty comes up in the discussion. Family members can count on the integrity of each other, through thick and thin. Just as God wrote, members of strong families live by the principle that "each of you must...speak truthfully,...for we are all members of one body."[17]

Now, we are not talking about the so-called honesty that borders on verbal abuse; nor are we discounting the importance of tact, the ability to keep one's mouth shut when words will do more harm than good. As we read in Ephesians 4:29, "Do not let any unwholesome talk come out of your mouths, but only what is helpful for building others up according to their needs, that it may benefit those who listen." We are simply saying that human beings in families (and everywhere else) need to be able to rely on the word of each other.

During a marriage enrichment seminar, one husband said this about his wife's honesty:

She's like a rock in that regard. I can always count on her to tell me what she is thinking. Fortunately, her interior self is as kind as her exterior self. She somehow has managed to become a person who holds few grudges and harbors little anger and resentment. I love her for it, and I strive to be as good and kind as she is, though I slip up on occasion. She's genuine!

CHARACTERISTIC #5—COMMITMENT TO FAMILY TRADITIONS

Traditions in families have been described as the *we always* of family life: *We always* have cider at Halloween. *We always* have hugs at bedtime. *We always...*

Family traditions serve an important role in family cohesiveness. You may recall one tradition of Jewish families that God began for them in the Old Testament. Each year at Passover, the eldest son was to ask, "What does this mean?" as the meal began.[18] The father responded with the story of God's deliverance of the Jews from Egyptian bondage. That wonderful family tradition not only kept the family unit focused on their religious heritage; it also bonded them together with memories of their special annual meal together.

Members of strong families often mentioned their family traditions.

We wanted our children to have a sense of who and where they are in history. We have continued traditions from my family and my wife's family. Oyster stew and carols on Christmas Eve are something we do, and the kids know that Grandma and Grandpa did it when they were young. That has to give a feeling of continuity.

I traced our family tree several years ago and am glad I did; but the list of names and dates wasn't very exciting to the kids. So we bought a tape recorder and asked older family members—grandparents, aunts, and uncles—to record what they remember: places they lived, occupations, how they celebrated holidays. We have also begun visiting areas where the family lived. We had good luck finding farms and old homes of grandparents and even great-grandparents, and we've used vacation time to visit some of those "home counties" and poke around in courthouse records and cemeteries for traces of family.

Each night when I put the baby down in his crib, I carry out a little ritual—even when he's asleep. I say, "Mama loves you. Daddy loves you. Your brother loves you. Grandmother loves you. You're a sweet, wonderful boy, and we're very glad you're with us."

When strong families make traditions—whether it's always having the evening meal together or an annual night of Christmas caroling—those traditions build an awareness of the unique and loving bond of each family member to the others.

CHARACTERISTIC #6—COMMITMENT TO THE LONG HAUL

Dependability is an important aspect of commitment in families. In a marriage enrichment workshop not long ago, the couples were talking about parenthood. "What's your greatest accomplishment as a father?" they asked a man with three children. His eyes grew wide, and he had a somewhat stricken look on his face as his mind did a fast rewind through countless memories. Finally, he choked out these words in a barely audible voice: "I hung in there."

The man, who by all indications was an excellent father, explained to the group that he and his family had faced many difficulties and genuine tragedies. Many times he'd wondered how he could possibly cope. He suddenly became misty-eyed in front of the whole group as he looked back over the years at how his family's commitment to each other had carried them through dark hours. And he was proud and grateful.

Strong families clearly reveal that commitment is for a long time. Over and over they said that they *expected* their family to endure.

We were reared to regard marriage as a till-death-do-us-part kind of arrangement. I can't say we'd never (never say never, you know) divorce, but we haven't considered it yet, and we've been married twenty-six years.

My son is in his last year of high school, and I'm facing the fact that my relationship with him is about to change quite a bit. He'll be out on his own, married, and with kids in a few years. I remind him that things may be different, but I'll still be his mother. That will not change.

A Rose by Any Other Name

You may have noticed that love is missing from the six secrets of strong families listed in the introduction. You may also have noticed that it's not in this chapter either. That's because too many people think of love as a feeling—butterflies in your tummy, tingles in your toes, fireworks when you kiss. And of course, those are wonderful feelings! It's great when your spouse's presence makes you feel all aglow. But real life has moments when you disagree and days when the kids drive you crazy. Moods fluctuate; feelings change.

Thus, the word *commitment* is used to describe a special kind of love—a love steady and sure that isn't subject to mood swings or the passage of years or hard times. It is a love that is conscious and unconditional. Commitment-love says, "I decide and promise to love you because of who you are, not what you do or how I feel."

Commitment describes the kind of love God commanded us to give him,[19] the kind of love he commanded a husband to have for his wife,[20] the kind he wants us to practice in our lives,[21] and certainly the kind of love on which all lasting relationships—even family relationships—are based.

In the gardens of Arbor Lodge, home of J. Sterling Morton, father of Arbor Day, is a monument with the poem that follows. It sums up commitment love quite nicely.

> Time flies.
> Flowers die.
> New days.
> New ways.
> Love stays.

Putting It to Work—Six Ideas for Your Family

1. *Have periodic family councils.* Ask family members, "How are we doing as a family? What needs to be changed? What are our family goals?"

2. *Renew your wedding vows.* Some couples have discovered a heightened sense of commitment by renewing their marriage vows. A wedding anniversary is a good time to do this. Choose a special location—a chapel or a garden, for example. Invite a few friends to witness the event and have an informal reception afterward. Wear your wedding dress or veil if you still have it (and fit into it!).

3. *Rearrange your schedules.* Is your family too busy? If everyone in the family gives up one activity, the family can gain much more time together. Or rearrange schedules so you can all be available at the same time. For example, Mom can move her meeting to Monday night while Junior is at soccer practice and Dad is out of town. Then everyone can be together Tuesday. Try to avoid Mom being out on Monday, Dad on Tuesday, and Junior on Wednesday.

4. *Examine your marriage relationship for danger signs* that may warn of an affair. We don't mean lipstick smears or mysterious phone calls; we mean signs that are visible before an affair begins. Dr. Carlfred Broderick, one of America's leading marriage counselors, calls these the three Rs of infidelity: resentment, rationalization, and rendezvous.

   ◆ *Resentment* involves any of the bad feelings or unresolved issues in a marriage that strain the relationship and make spouses vulnerable to temptation.

   ◆ *Rationalization* is a process that most people in adulterous situations go through. "She needs my help; we need time alone to discuss things." "His wife doesn't understand him like I do. I only want to hold him and comfort him."

- *Rendezvous* describes those opportunities that make an affair much more likely—candlelight dinners, traveling together to conventions, long hours working together.

Couples who are serious about guarding against infidelity can be sure to keep resentment cleared away. They can learn to recognize rationalization for what it is, and they can avoid rendezvous opportunities.

5. *Read good books as a family.* Read Alex Haley's *Roots*, Louisa May Alcott's *Little Women* or *Little Men*, Lew Wallace's *Ben Hur*, or Pearl Buck's *The Good Earth* together. Or read them individually and discuss them. These stories deal with commitment in relationships and can stimulate discussion about commitment with your children. Laura Ingalls Wilder's *Little House on the Prairie* and other books are suitable for younger readers.

6. *Rent movies that deal with commitment* in relationships or examples of good family life. *Heidi, Fiddler on the Roof, Little House on the Prairie,* and *Our Town* are some examples. Watch your selections together, have popcorn or cookies, and then talk about what you have seen. What did these families do that was good? How are we like them?

STEP TWO

EXPRESS APPRECIATION
AND AFFECTION

I had to sit by his graveside and tell him I forgave him before I could go on with my life," Lane quietly confided. "Sounds strange, huh? But I didn't know what else to do. All the time I was growing up, I never seemed to be able to live up to his standards. I tried hard. Made the best grades I could. Got onto the varsity team by sheer hustle and attitude and started every game. I wasn't a star, but I was steady, and I gave it 100 percent.

"But he never noticed. Or at least he never said anything if he did.

"All I ever heard from him was what I'd done wrong or how I could do better next time. I never heard a 'You did good, Son' or an 'I'm proud of you, Son' anytime in my life. As far as I know, my dad didn't care much for me. He gave me a roof over my head and made sure there was food on the table. And I guess I should be happy for that. Some never had that much. But the thing I wanted most—the thing I never got—was to *know* that he loved me. I wanted him to say he loved me and to say other things that gave proof to those words. I wanted his approval.

"A couple of years after he died, I realized how much never hearing those things from my dad affected the way I lived and how driven

I was to succeed at everything I did. I was so driven that I neglected my wife. And my own son.

"I finally figured out that since he was dead, I would never hear him say those kinds of things to me—no matter how successful I was. Oh, I knew that in my head the day he died. But it took me two years to believe it in my heart.

"So I drove to the cemetery and sat by his grave. I knew he wasn't there, but I wasn't doing it for him. I told him how much I hurt and how confused my life had gotten. I told him how hard I'd tried to win his affection and appreciation and how nothing I did was ever enough. I told him that because I was *still* trying to get his approval, I was failing my wife and my boy. Then I told him that I was going to be a better father than he had been. I wouldn't just put bread on the table and clothes on their backs. I would be on the lookout for reasons to say nice things about them, and I would make sure that from that day forward my wife and my son would know *every day of their lives* just how much I loved them.

"I said, 'Dad, I forgive you. But I'm never gonna be like you. At least not in this way. My boy'll never have to forgive me one day for not making him feel special and loved.'

"Then I walked back to my car and drove away. I've done just what I said, and I always will. My family will always hear about every good thing I see in them and every warm feeling I have for them. Always and forever."

Lane had done what he needed to do and had done it well. He knew from deep within himself that one of the most important things a family can do to be strong, happy, and loving is to express all the affection and appreciation it can.

A SURPRISING DISCOVERY

Many of the results of the family-strengths research were somewhat anticipated. However, one discovery came as quite a surprise. As the data from the questionnaires and interviews were analyzed, the importance of appreciation and affection surfaced again and again.

Expressions of appreciation and affection *permeated* relationships within strong families. They let each other know on a daily basis that each is appreciated.

So often when we watch TV or a movie, my wife will say to me, "I'm glad you are the way you are. You're good to me and the kids; you don't drink; you're not so wrapped up in work that nothing else matters."

He sends me a big bouquet of white daisies with one yellow daisy and a note that reads, "You're one in a million."

This sounds too simple, but Marie thanks me for everyday things that I do. If, for example, I fold the laundry, she thanks me. This helps me know that I'm not taken for granted.

He makes me feel good about me and about us as a couple. Very few days go by that he doesn't say something like "You look really nice today" or "The house is so clean and comfortable; it's a real pleasure to be home" or "I enjoyed our working together on this project; we're a great team."

Each night before we go to sleep, we tell each other, "I love you." Sometimes it isn't easy when we've had a spat or a bad day, but we still say it—and mean it.

This shouldn't be so surprising, should it? Even God made it clear that he wants to be appreciated and told of that appreciation. On one occasion, Jesus heard the pleas of ten lepers who cried out for healing. Taking compassion on them, he instructed them to go show themselves to the priest because, under the law, lepers could only be considered clean if a priest pronounced them clean. As they searched out the priest, God gave them a miracle—he healed them. All ten were healed, but only one came back to say thank you.

> One of them, when he saw he was healed, came back, praising God in a loud voice. He threw himself at Jesus' feet and thanked him—and he was a Samaritan.

Jesus asked, "Were not all ten cleansed? Where are the other nine? Was no one found to return and give praise to God except this foreigner?" Then he said to him, "Rise and go; your faith has made you well."[1]

Jesus made it very clear that he expected expressed appreciation and that he was pleased with the one who gave it. He indicated just as clearly his disappointment in those nine who didn't return to thank him for what he had done.

INTELLECT AND EMOTION

The Bible teaches it, and strong families confirmed it. Appreciation is a vital characteristic of strong families. But there is something more. Earlier models of family strengths discussed appreciation alone. Today, we think in terms of both appreciation *and* affection.

The distinction is important.

Appreciation can be extended on a purely intellectual level—without any emotion, without genuine feeling. It can be something we say or do in honor of another person because we see an advantage in doing it. Affection, however, is more than that. It is clearly an *emotional* response. An empty "good job" or a pat on the shoulder doesn't carry much weight, but with the added emotional component of affection, expressed appreciation becomes very powerful. In other words, the expression of appreciation needs to be real and genuine.

Many of the strong families in the family-strengths research exhibit a wonderful blend of intellect and emotion in action. They not only give appreciation, but they do it with affection. On seeing them interact in their natural environment, the observer is struck by the positive "electricity" that fills the room, and he or she quickly concludes: "These folks genuinely like each other! They like to be together. They feel deeply and strongly for each other."

Jesus aptly defined the depths of affection when he said, "Love the Lord your God with all your heart and with all your soul and with all your mind."[2]

Surely a person who loves like that will also love with his arms (hugs) and vocal chords (expressed appreciation), don't you think?

WHY WE DO WHAT WE DO

"I think you're overemphasizing this," you may be thinking. "My family knows how much I appreciate them, but they also know that I'm the quiet type. What you're saying is okay for extroverts, but not us introverts. It isn't necessary for people like me to continually express affection."

Oh, but it is necessary for people like you! Very necessary. It's necessary no matter what your temperament or nature. Some students of human nature argue convincingly that the need to be appreciated is one of the most important of all human needs. Think about it. Why do we work so hard all our lives? Why do we take second jobs or work overtime to get braces on the kids' teeth? Or paint the front of the house? Or get a degree?

Money, of course, is an important motivation. Prestige and ego might be others. But there's something deeper going on, because people with more than enough money to live and more than enough prestige to be famous *still* do things for others. In spite of all that we own or have accomplished, we keep pushing ourselves. The pleasure of owning a fancy camera or a designer coat or an all-leather couch with real oak armrests can't be so great that we'd want to wear ourselves out pursuing them, can it?

No! More often than not, it's appreciation that we're really after. We want the kids to smile through straight front teeth and say they love us for all those wires and rubber bands. We want our spouses to recognize and be grateful for the hard hours we work to care for the kids, yard, house, and/or to provide income. We want to be valued for who we are and what we do.

Valued!

That's the important thing here.

When a person expresses appreciation to another, he or she in essence says, "You are a person of worth and dignity. I am interested in you and am aware of your positive qualities. I affirm who you are as well as what you have done."

That is a powerful message.

When we receive that kind of appreciation from others, it enhances our self-worth. As Dr. Don Clifton, a psychologist, puts it, appreciation fills our bucket (of self-esteem). But with that interesting and seemingly accurate analogy, there is something very important to remember. A person's bucket is harder to fill than it is to empty! Besides that, it tips over easily! As one of the strong family members said,

> If somebody puts you down, they've got their dipper in your bucket. By my estimate, it takes about ten positive strokes to repair the damage of one negative.

Many unhappy families have bucket and dipper problems. Spouses can't seem to say anything good about each other; parents criticize and belittle the children. Good families, however, have learned to *fill* those esteem buckets. A Kansas wife said,

> My husband talks positively about me to others. Some of his coworkers say bad things about their spouses. This makes him quite angry and all the more mindful of saying only nice things about me. Those other jerks hurt their wives and their relationships by their offensive behavior, but they unwittingly make my life more wonderful as my husband goes out of his way to tell people all the good things he can about me!

Another woman was especially touched when, as she explained,

> My daughter wrote me a letter after her baby was born and said, "I hope I can be as good a mom as you are." That really made my day, my week, my month! I'll never throw out that letter. I know I made mistakes as a mother. So does my daughter! But all she chooses to remember and to affirm in me are the things I did right. I can't begin to tell you what that means to me.

One daughter in Germany told us,

Every Saturday my father goes to market, and he always brings home some beautiful flowers for my mother. It is really a sweet thing for him to do, and it makes my mother feel like a queen. The flowers have been a tradition since I was a child. Everyone in the family looks forward to them.

THE RIPPLE EFFECT

These strong families demonstrate that appreciation and affection help family members grow and flourish as each person's self-esteem is boosted. As a pebble dropped in a pond causes ripples all around, so pebbles of appreciation cause ripples that carry into other facets of life. The family becomes a fun place to be, and the environment of love makes everything better.

A WARM, HOSPITABLE ENVIRONMENT

When Dr. John DeFrain—one of the primary contributors to the family-strengths research—and his family were in the South Pacific studying family strengths and challenges on a Fulbright Scholarship, they lived in Deuba, Fiji, and had many Fijian friends. One of their best family friends was the Talemaigau family: Eroni, the father; Mereani, the mother; and five young children. The Fijian culture values kindness, sharing, caring, being happy, not clouding one's days with worry, being respectful, and feeling safe and secure. John DeFrain and Eroni spent many late afternoons together after work, sitting on the verandah of the DeFrains' house.

"We talked a bit, back and forth, telling about the two different worlds we came from. Fiji clearly is not Nebraska!" John explained. "But a lot of the time we would just sit silently, enjoying the afternoon—the sun and the birds and the wind—and enjoying each other's company.

"I didn't know many Fijian words, and Eroni spoke an interesting blend of British English with a Fijian accent that sometimes was mystifying to American ears. But in spite of this, we communicated well with each other.

"Not long after we were settled in Fiji, our Seattle friends, Jeff and Sandi and daughter Jessica, arrived for a short visit. Jeff went out late one afternoon for a session with Eroni on the verandah. When Eroni went home two hours later, Jeff walked into the house smiling and delighted. 'Gosh! I sure love that Eroni! You know,' he paused thoughtfully, 'I can hardly understand a word Eroni says, but he sure is fun to be with.'

"That may be the secret to the South Pacific," John concluded. "Fijians know how to simply *be*. When they come to visit, and they come to visit all the time, you don't have to entertain them. You don't have to tell stories or perform or 'host' their visit. You can simply enjoy being with them, sharing the joy of human beings being together—nothing more, nothing less. A close bond develops among people who enjoy and appreciate each other's company."

Perhaps families could learn to create that same sense of "fun to be with" if they created the same environment of appreciation and affection. Families who've created this type of atmosphere in their homes find themselves going out of their way to make things happier, easier, and less stressful for each other.

I have been confined to our home for several years now due to an illness. I can go out only rarely and then only in a wheelchair. Not long ago, I was having an especially bad time, very ill—and it was near my birthday. I've always been fond of bagpipe music; I guess that's just a little strange! My husband found someone in town who plays bagpipes and arranged for him to come over to our home. He stood outside my window and played a private little concert for me. Did I mention this was a surprise? I'll bet the neighbors never forget it either.

You asked what my spouse does that makes me feel good. Well, I'll tell you. She doesn't harp on my faults and shortcomings. Being a human, I have a few. She remembers my accomplishments, good deeds, and pluses. Sometimes I forget them, and she reminds me I'm a pretty decent guy.

Our daughter takes violin lessons from a teacher who uses the Suzuki method. I have been influenced by the experience too. Her teacher is rarely critical of how she plays. Instead she'll say, "Your posture is nice today; now, if you'll move this finger more this direction, the notes will sound better." I've tried applying the technique at home, and it works there too. Instead of "Jessie, I asked you to tidy your room and you only did half of it," I'll say, "Jessie, the work you did on your room helped the way it looks. Now come back and finish it." We're both happier! No yelling, fussing, cajoling, or frustration on anyone's part. We just love each other and stay at things until they get done.

As you might guess from these examples, appreciation and affection help to keep the atmosphere pleasant and positive. This is not surprising; we all prefer to be with people who make us feel good about ourselves.

A BETTER SEX LIFE

Another ripple effect of appreciation reported by the folks in the family-strengths research is that they enjoy healthy sex lives. They weren't asked how many times they have intercourse each week or what techniques they use. Neither of these would be real indicators of the vitality of their sexual relationships. The people in these strong families confirm this feeling:

After all the years we've been married, she can still kiss me and make my heart skip a beat.

We bought one of those sex manuals once out of curiosity and a notion we might be missing something. What a hoot it was! Besides some information that I question, it was so mechanical. It made sex seem very difficult—not at all fun or even sexy.

Our sex life gets better every year that goes by. We may not make love as often as we did in the first years of marriage, but the intensity of feeling is much greater.

The quality of the sexual relationship is a reflection of the quality of the total relationship. Without goodwill, fostered by appreciation in all areas of family life, the atmosphere is not suitable for a healthy sex life.

Obviously God intends that a good sexual realationship be part of marriage. He even made it a part of the marital contract.

> The husband should fulfill his marital duty to his wife, and likewise the wife to her husband. The wife's body does not belong to her alone but also to her husband. In the same way, the husband's body does not belong to him alone but also to his wife. Do not deprive each other except by mutual consent and for a time, so that you may devote yourselves to prayer. Then come together again so that Satan will not tempt you because of your lack of self-control.[3]

In the context of this passage, "marital duty" means sexual fulfillment. It comes from a Koine Greek word that means *obligation*. God says that we are obligated to satisfy our spouses sexually. But just as appreciation feels empty without affection, so does sex without affection. We need sexual fulfillment, but we want that fulfillment to be part of our love and affection for each other.

When you think about it like that, you realize that sex doesn't begin at 10:30 Saturday night with a shower and perfume. You've got to start early. Not even at 7:30 with a dinner by candlelight. You've got to start *really* early. Try starting Monday morning by taking out the garbage and Tuesday afternoon by complimenting your spouse on a job well done.

Sexual fulfillment isn't just sex. It's a wonderful environment of love, appreciation, and affection that permeates the home. When that environment is there, sex is never "just sex." It's the culmination of a husband and wife loving each other in every way—body, mind, and spirit.

Strong families are aware of the value of this total approach.

The times when sex was best have been times when my wife and I felt especially close and in tune with each other—when we've solved a problem or when we're working on a project together.

I learned a long time ago that I can't gripe about my husband's sloppy ways, insinuate that he doesn't bring home enough money, drool over some hunk on TV, and still expect him [my husband] to be thrilled with me.

WHY SOME HAVE DIFFICULTY SHOWING AFFECTION

Appreciation and affection are so crucial to strong families, but not everyone knows how to express them in productive and beneficial ways. Read again the story at the beginning of this chapter to see how devastating unexpressed love can be.

What keeps people from knowing how to show affection and express appreciation?

For some, it's a matter of culture. In some cultures and subcultures, the expression of emotion is frowned upon, while in others it is encouraged. Our so-called "male culture" in the U.S. tends to be less emotional than our "female culture," and most men would think twice about showing affection in public. However, in some European and third-world cultures, men show affection without inhibition. In those cultures, even the most "macho" of men are allowed and encouraged to express appreciation and affection without hesitation or embarrassment.

Sometimes it isn't culture that inhibits the display of affection; it's the home in which one grew up. Joe Beam came from a home that wasn't very touchy-feely, while his wife, Alice, came from a home where people hugged freely and frequently. It isn't unusual in America for people from very different families of origin to marry each other and bring with them very different ideas about how appreciation and affection should be expressed.

With the combined impact of culture and early family example, some people have serious hurdles to overcome before they can learn how to express appreciation and affection. And this seems to be truer of males than females in our society.

Even with such hurdles to overcome, big, strong men tend to enjoy affection and quickly learn (from their more expressive wives) the benefits of genuine emotional touch, as the following story shows.

"His family was pretty stunted in terms of expressing affection," Sheryl explained as Brandon smiled and nodded in agreement. "The first time he met my family at Thanksgiving dinner, I thought he would pass out. Everybody was hugging and laughing and having a great time."

"Yeah," Brandon added. "My family's idea of a good time was having an intellectual debate over welfare reform. Soon we'd all be in a big argument and somebody would storm out the door."

"After a few years of 'therapy' in my family, he came around," Sheryl said. "I don't want to make him sound like a troubled soul, of course. He's a very rational guy and helps keep me on an even keel. He can sit down and analyze a situation and figure out step-by-step how to get through it. I really need that from him. But he's also learned how to be loving and affectionate. How to give hugs and compliments and to say warm, cuddly things to me. I need that from him too."

"Yes, you do," chided Brandon. So she poked him in the ribs to get even as they both laughed.

Six Secrets to Cultivating Appreciation and Affection in Your Home

Brandon isn't the only man who's learned the value of affection. In the thousands of couples who've gone through Family Dynamics Institute's *His Needs, Her Needs* course, many men have learned how to enjoy showing more affection to their wives. In that course, each couple completes an inventory that helps each mate determine his or her most important emotional needs. Most often, it's the wife who needs more affection and the husband who learns to enjoy giving it to her in ample quantities. It's not unusual, though, for a husband to discover that he needs more affection, and so his wife learns how to wrap him in a blanket of affection that changes both their lives.

You, too, can have a home filled with affection and appreciation. Following are six secrets for incorporating these qualities into *your* family.

SECRET #1—DIG FOR DIAMONDS

Liberal amounts of appreciation and affection do much to improve and strengthen family life. Many of us, however, have difficulties in either expressing or receiving appreciation. One reason we have problems showing appreciation is that we haven't learned to be good miners.

South African diamond miners spend their working lives sifting through thousands of tons of rock and dirt looking for a few tiny diamonds. They know that what they're going to find in those tons of dirt will more than compensate all their efforts to find it. Too often in family relationships, people tend to do just the opposite. They sweep aside the diamonds, eagerly searching for dirt. However, members of healthy families are diamond experts. They look for the good in each other.

My husband is the classic "absent-minded professor" type who tends to forget birthdays and such. But there are other ways he shows he loves me. Last week, he saw kiefels [a kind of Croatian or Czech roll] in a Czech bakery and bought them for me because he knows how much I like them—and how hard they are to find. It made me remember again that when he forgets, it isn't because he doesn't love me. This year, rather than seeing his love in a birthday card, I saw it in a kiefel!

I ran my first marathon last week and finished fifteenth out of seventy-nine runners in my age group (fifteen to twenty years). I was disappointed at not being first and was thinking how fourteen guys came in ahead of me. Then Mom reminded me that sixty-four came in after me! She helped me see how I'd won instead of how I'd lost. She made me feel really special.

Psychologists talk about self-fulfilling prophecies. This is a fancy way of saying that you pretty much get what you're looking for in life. If you choose to follow a dismal path, you'll have your unhappy dreams fulfilled time and time again. If you search for the bad in other members of your family, you can discover that, too, and have a miserable family life. But here's better news: If you look for the good in your family, you'll certainly find it and have a happy family life.

We fell into a trap early in our marriage—partly because of some other couples we saw socially. They considered themselves to be very sophisticated, and nothing or no one quite measured up to their standards. One particular couple delighted in acid sarcasm—especially with each other.

We didn't realize how we were being affected until we left town for a three-week vacation. Soon, we felt relaxed and happy and assumed it was the trip that had made us feel better. We came back to town feeling good, went to a party at our friends' house, and came home in a depression. We were puzzled.

The next day we sat down to figure things out. We analyzed what was going on. The sarcasm, fault-finding, and belittling were rubbing off on us. It had been a subtle process, but we had begun to see things in a negative way. It was affecting our marriage too.

We decided to stop. Our first step was to find some new couples to socialize with. We also worked on our attitudes. We chose to accent the positive.

Now when my husband comes home, he says, "Wow! You've been busy with the boys today, got your hair cut, and did the marketing." He doesn't even mention the weedy garden. And when he comes in disappointed over a sale he missed, I remind him of the three he made last week. We have conditioned ourselves to look at what we have, what we have completed, and what we are rather than what we lack, what isn't done, and what we can't be.

Share the Diamonds You Mine with the One You Mine Them From

Another reason people express appreciation so infrequently is that they have low self-esteem. While homes that practice appreciation and affection tend to promote healthy self-esteem, even members of those homes have times when they question their value. The way to help those family members is to keep digging for the diamonds! One Nevada mother shared this:

> *Our daughter is having trouble right now with acne and other changes in growing up. She feels ugly and clumsy. To compensate, she had begun demeaning other girls and boys by talking about how bad Janie's skin is or how fat Elly is or how awkward Bill is. We don't like her behaving this way, so we have emphasized to her that she'll grow out of this phase. We have tried to get her to focus on her good points. I bought ribbons and barrettes and fancy combs because her hair is gorgeous. We refuse to let her put others down, and we balance her comments. For example, if she says Elly is fat, we say, "She'll grow up too. In the meantime, she is an excellent student and musician."*

This mother is doing the right thing. She is digging for diamonds in her daughter and others, then showing her daughter the beautiful jewels she finds. She helps her daughter see the good in both herself and her friends.

When we don't feel good about ourselves, it is difficult to feel good about others. The Bible makes this very clear. One of the New Testament's most repeated phrases is "Love your neighbor as yourself."[4] A person who refuses to see the good and value in self cannot see the good and value in others.

In dealing with people who lack self-esteem, it is important to be positive. Teach them subtly how to show regard for others by showing appreciation for them. This is not an easy task, for some people can be quite obnoxious. They are a challenge to love and appreciate. But remember, as they learn to experience the joy of a healthy self-esteem, they can learn to appreciate others as well.

Express Appreciation Truthfully

We often are hesitant to show admiration for others because we think they may feel we are insincere or have ulterior motives. One California wife said it this way:

Now, if I told my husband that he is a wonderful mechanic, he'd know I was lying. But he is a wonderful dad to our sons. He spends hours with them. They go to all the construction sites to watch the cranes and bulldozers. Not all dads are like that.

A father from New England said,

I hate to hear people being phony in talking with children. I believe in praising mine, but I give them credit for some brains too. I don't say, "You jump higher than anyone" to my six-year-old. She knows better. I say, "You can jump so high. You're doing good."

Another man said this:

At first, some people are skeptical of my expressions of appreciation. I can tell they're wondering what I'm after. But with time, I think that my sincerity becomes apparent because I'm careful not to use false flattery. If I don't mean it, I don't say it.

Members of strong families realize that it isn't necessary to be insincere in expressing appreciation, because each person has many good qualities and accomplishments. They all believe that if someone makes us feel good we should let them know.

SECRET #2—AFFIRM YOUR CHILDREN VERBALLY

A wonderful way to nurture an atmosphere of affection and appreciation in the home is to teach children their value from the very day they are born. As parents, we literally mold good or bad people out of our babies by telling them they are good or bad. We teach them self-esteem through our appreciation. The children in strong families who were old enough to respond reflected this in their comments.

I like to read, and Mom and Dad are always happy when I finish another book. Sometimes they give me a treat, like going out for pizza.

My big brother, Josh, and I were playing catch, and I was catching lots of times. Josh said, "Wow! Wherever I throw the ball, David catches it." That was last summer, and I still like to think about it.

My family moved from Oregon to Mississippi last year. We had to rent a truck, pack it, and do everything ourselves. I've never worked so hard or sweated so much. But my parents told me that they couldn't have done it without me. I overheard them telling other people too. I feel really proud of myself.

Pablo Casals, world-famous cellist and recipient of the U.S. Presidential Medal of Freedom, shares some thoughts on what we teach children:

> Each second we live in a new and unique moment of the universe, a moment that never was before and never will be again. And what do we teach our children in school? We teach them that two and two make four, and that Paris is the capital of France. Will we also teach them what they are?
>
> We should say to each of them, "Do you know what you are? You are a marvel. You are unique. In all the world there is no other child exactly like you.... And look at your body—what a wonder it is! Your legs, your arms, your cunning fingers, the way you move! You may become a Shakespeare, a Michelangelo, a Beethoven. You have the capacity for anything."[5]

If we want true affection in our homes, we must teach it to our children by verbally affirming just how loveable and special they are—every chance we get!

SECRET #3—EXPECT CHILDREN TO BE AFFECTIONATE AND APPRECIATIVE

Another thing good families have taught us is that children can learn from an early age to express appreciation. Initially, children learn from the example of their parents and by performing simple tasks of showing their gratitude to others. Gradually, they build a foundation from which they see the good qualities of others and feel comfortable about showing their appreciation for those qualities.

As one father in Alabama said,

Many people don't bother to teach children even basic manners such as saying "Thank you." They think children are too young to learn such things. But that isn't so. My wife and I use good manners with each other and our children in everyday life. Our older son, when he was only about two, would say "dee doo" for "thank you."

Nancy Stinnett tells us about a bright, beautiful sixteen-month-old Korean child named Yeeun who was in the Infant Laboratory at the University of Alabama. "Even though she is very young, her parents have already taught her to give a little bow to her teacher when she leaves each day. It is a sign of her respect to an elder and a sign of her gratitude to a teacher. And she is absolutely charming!"

A teen from Colorado told us,

M*y parents gave me some note cards when I was quite young. I think they had a tree frog design on them, but they were for me to use to write thank-you notes. Whenever I received a gift, I was expected to write a note to thank whoever gave it to me. If a friend's parents took me with their family to the zoo or the circus, I wrote a note. My parents reminded me if I neglected this.*

It has been suggested that showing our appreciation and gratitude to others is as important to their well-being as water is to flowers. Children can be taught to water the flowers. The sooner they are taught, the happier the family can be.

SECRET #4—SHARE HUMOR AND PLAYFULNESS

Playfulness and humor are important aspects of appreciation and affection. Families express their feelings for each other by having fun together. Dr. Jon Wuerffel, an air force chaplain, was convinced humor was a family strength and did an excellent study that showed this.

Jon first looked at the research on the psychology of humor and found that humor is used in many ways, both positively and negatively. Then he carefully studied the issue with 304 mothers, fathers, and their teenaged children at the Air Force Academy in Colorado Springs. He statistically related these families' use of humor to their other family strengths. Basically, he was asking, will strong families be funny families?

The answer: Yes.

Strong families tend to use a lot of *positive* humor. They enjoy each other's company, they like to laugh and tell stories, they like to play together, and they express affection with gentle humor. But two kinds of humor—sarcasm and put-downs—are not related to strong families. In fact, the term *negative humor* is misleading. Sarcasm and put-downs are not humor at all. They are verbal weapons used to dominate people, show power, and establish control.

Jon was so moved by the study that he sheepishly vowed to change some of his ways. "In high school I learned about sarcasm and put-downs in the locker room. I was a quarterback on the football team, and you had to be quick-witted verbally to avoid being smeared by the other guys.

"I was always good at cutting everybody down, and I think I mistook sarcasm for genuine humor. When I saw the results of my research, I instantly felt ashamed.

"In fact, I went to Lola [his good-humored wife] and asked her, 'Am I really a bit too sarcastic sometimes?' She let me know in a kindly manner that I was, indeed, too sarcastic sometimes. I'm striving to do better now, for I know what genuine humor is."

Don't you wish American television and movie writers and producers would learn what genuine, helpful, family-building humor is? Knowing what we know, it is dismaying to watch a movie or television show that models stupid, destructive types of humor. Sarcasm and put-downs dominate on-screen interchanges and no doubt seep into off-screen private life.

Forgo negative "humor" and let loose with all the warm-hearted, fun-loving humor you can muster. Share the stories that live through the years and still make everyone laugh. Stories like when Grandpa accidentally shot at the cow when he thought it was a mountain lion and how it got so frightened it wouldn't give milk for a week. Every family has stories like these, and more are made every year. Learn to laugh with each other and watch the long-term effect it has on the level of affection in your family.

Just remember, don't share stories that sting or embarrass. The point is to laugh together, all having a good time, not to put down or humiliate—even in the slightest.

SECRET #5—PURPOSELY ENCOURAGE AFFECTION AND APPRECIATION

Life might be simpler if we could pass a law that required regular displays of appreciation and affection within families. That, of course, isn't possible. Members of strong families have discovered, however, that expressions of appreciation and affection can be encouraged.

During the first two years of our marriage, my husband was good about remembering our anniversary and my birthday. Then he sort of began to fade out. When he forgot our third-anniversary, I was quite upset and cried all night. He brought me long-stemmed roses the next day, but I felt as if he'd only done it because I'd made a fuss.

In the next several years, he forgot several anniversaries and birthdays, and we had a repeat of that third-anniversary scene. I'd cry or become angry, and he'd come in later with flowers or candy or some other gift. At a friend's suggestion, I decided to try a different approach.

Here's what I do now: I begin pointing out the approach of special events ahead of time. I do it casually and in good humor. I'll say something like "That new Italian restaurant would be perfect to celebrate our anniversary next week" or "Do you think your mom would watch the girls so we could do something special for my birthday—which is coming up soon?"

I guess you could call those heavy hints. I will say that they've done the job. Jim hasn't missed a birthday or anniversary since I changed tactics. Some folks might not approve, I suppose. But it seems Jim needs the reminder. He's absent-minded about other things, so I know it isn't anything personal. We both feel better now. I don't feel forgotten or unloved, and he doesn't end up in a no-win situation.

Some might feel uncomfortable with this woman's approach, but we encourage you to think about it just a moment. If your husband or wife were absent-minded or forgetful, would you mind if his or her secretary dropped a reminder about your birthday? What about your mate's mother? For most, the answers to either of those questions would be, "Well, that would be okay." So you see, you're not upset with the fact that your spouse needs reminding; it's the fact that you feel less than special if *you* have to do the reminding! If that's the case, ask someone else to do the reminding. Remember the point from a few pages ago: Don't look for the negative; look for the good. Dig for the diamonds. And one very important way to do that is to purposely encourage others in your family to show appropriate manifestations of appreciation and affection.

The brother of one of the authors of this book (we'll hide his identity for his own protection) calls him whenever anyone in their family of origin—father, mother, brother, sister—has a birthday. The forgetful guy is asked, "Do you know whose birthday it is today?" When the calling brother inevitably hears a negative reply, he continues, "It's Mother's [or whosever], and I just thought you might want to give her a call."

Everybody feels good about the outcome. Mother feels good about getting the call. The forgetful brother feels good that he didn't miss the special day. The reminding brother not only gets a good feeling from knowing he helped his brother and mother; he also gets something else to good-naturedly rib his brother about for the next couple of months over lunch!

SECRET #6—ACCEPT EXPRESSIONS OF APPRECIATION GRACEFULLY

We've all had it happen to us. Someone does something you like or looks especially nice and you say, "Your speech was excellent" or "That suit is beautiful." And the recipient of your praise replies, "I thought it was too long" or "This old thing? I hate it."

And there you stand, feeling stupid.

Members of our strong families realize that the ability to receive appreciation gracefully is critical to keeping the appreciation flowing.

My wife grew up in a family where compliments were scarce. Whenever I'd praise her—on her cooking, for example—she'd say, "I know you like it, because you ate it." I'd say, "Yes, but I like to tell you, anyway." In time, she has learned how to accept praise; and as she learned how to accept it, she learned how to give it as well.

Our twins have hit that awkward pre-teen stage; they don't know how they want to behave. They eat it up when someone admires their clothes or tells them they've done a good job in ballet. And yet they're embarrassed. They don't want to appear to be puffed up, so they sometimes are silly and giggle or say the wrong thing. We're helping them learn some correct ways to accept a compliment. We have even practiced with them. They find that hilarious, but it has helped them be more gracious.

Many of us are uncomfortable as the recipients of praise or compliments. We don't wish to appear immodest or don't care for the spotlight. Not accepting expressions of gratitude or appreciation correctly, however, can be interpreted as a rebuff and may stymie future overtures of appreciation. One Georgia woman remarked,

I regard it as tacky to wipe out a compliment by saying something contrary to it. I have some responses I like to give when someone compliments me—depending on the circumstances, of course. I might say, "Thank you for telling me (I did a good job or sang well or whatever)" or "It's sweet of you to notice." I try to phrase my response in a way that compliments them in return.

That works not only with those outside the family but also with those in the family. How would it make your child feel if when she says, "I love you," you reply, "How could you love someone like me?" That kind of response doesn't nurture security and happiness in a child; it only confuses and bewilders. The parent may say something like that because he or she is having a bad day or feeling especially unlovable, but that shouldn't be an excuse to cause harm to a child's need for reassurance and stability. Whenever any child compliments a mother or father, that compliment should be accepted as if it were the most wonderful thing in the world. When you accept your children's compliments with grace and a total belief in their sincerity, they're much more likely to receive your appreciation and affection the same way.

Children also watch how Mom and Dad receive the compliments and kindnesses passed between each other. Kids don't want to have to wonder what is true and what is not. They want sincerity and want both the giving and receiving of niceties to be sincere.

So for the sake of yourself and your family, receive expressions of affection and appreciation with a sweet, gentle grace.

A FINAL COMMENT

In marriage-enrichment workshops, couples are often given an exercise in which they are instructed to verbally express appreciation to each other. They are asked to make lists of each other's good qualities and to read their lists to each other in front of the group. The men often have big lumps in their throats and the women's eyes glisten. And as they finish and sit down to give another couple their spot in the limelight, they may protest, "Shucks, she [or he] knows all this stuff!" But even if she or he does know it, it doesn't hurt to hear it once more.

Homework assignments are sometimes given at the seminars. One such assignment is for the participants to create something special for their spouses—something that expresses the appreciation and affection they have for each other. Some make a special card or write a letter; others paint a picture or compose a song or poem. The idea is to give something creative and personal that is a little gift of yourself to someone who is very special to you.

Workshop participants come back to report marvelously creative acts. One woman came up beaming after class one evening. "Look at my new locket," she smiled, holding up a gold necklace with a heart-shaped locket. Carefully, she opened the locket to reveal a tiny scroll inside.

"Remember when we wrote down all the great things we liked about our partners and then read the list to each other in front of the group? Remember how choked up I got?"

Everyone remembered.

"Well, Dan went out and had a calligrapher write all the qualities he appreciated in me on this tiny scroll. Then he tied a tiny bow around the scroll and put it in this locket. I can't believe how creative he was."

What a husband!

Expressions of appreciation and affection are like good music. We can listen to them again and again.

Putting It to Work—Six Ideas for Your Family

1. *Write down ten things you like about your spouse.* (Five will do if you can't come up with ten right now.) Be specific. Say, "I like the sparkle in your eyes" rather than "You're nice-looking." No mixed messages, such as "I like you, even though you're a butterball." Don't put all your emphasis on accomplishments. Remember to appreciate people for what they are (patient, loving, fun to be with, gentle) as well as what they do. Share these with your spouse. The same technique can be used with children, parents, in-laws, and other folks. You can be creative in doing this exercise. One young woman had her father's positive characteristics inscribed on a photograph he loved. Other people make this a game while they're traveling: "Okay, let's all go around the car and each one of us will tell what we like about everyone in the car, one at a time."

2. *Create a positive, pleasant environment in your home.* One way to do this is to begin rephrasing negative, critical statements in positive ways. For example, you don't have to say to your child, "You fool, you spilled pop all over the table." You can say, "Whoops! Get a rag and we'll wipe it up." You don't have to say to your husband,

"Slow down, you animal. I'm not ready!" You can say, "How about a good back rub and leg massage? That gets me in a warm and friendly mood." For nearly every negative statement, you can come up with a way to rephrase it positively.

3. *Try reframing the situation.* This is a technique involving mental gymnastics. Many faults we see in ourselves and others are really positive qualities carried to an extreme. For example, the spouse who is stingy is really only a thrifty person in the extreme. Is your child loud and out of control, or enthusiastic? Granted, the enthusiasm may need some curbing and the tightwad may need to loosen the grip on the dollar. The point is that we view that person differently when we can see the core of good. Select two or three traits of your spouse or children that annoy you or that are negative. Redefine them in positive terms. Here are a few examples to get you started:

Spendthrift/Wastes money ......versus ....Generous

Talks too much/Chatters ....versus ....Likes to share

Domineering/Bossy ....versus ....Leadership

Always into things/Messy ....versus ....Curious

Won't follow rules/Messy ....versus ....Creative

Nitpicking ....versus ....Attentive to detail

Meddlesome/Interfering ....versus ....Interested/Concerned

4. *Encourage appreciation by receiving it gracefully.* It isn't necessary to say anything elaborate in return to someone who compliments you. A simple "Thank you" is often sufficient, or you might say, "I appreciate your sharing that with me" or "You're very kind" or "What a nice thing to say." You won't appear haughty by doing so; you will make the person complimenting you feel good.

5. *Give one compliment per day to your spouse and kids.* Make it a daily goal. Some people find it helpful to use a chart to remind themselves and to keep track of their progress. Although a bit mechanical, the chart can be an aid in getting the new behavior

established. As expressing appreciation and affection becomes a habit, you won't need the chart.

6. *Write birthday letters expressing your love.* Each year on your spouse or child's birthday, give them a personal letter. In it you can reminisce about things you did together during the past year and tell them what you're especially proud of them for. Include a list of things they did or traits they possess that make you love them. This is a good self-esteem builder for the receiver and a foundation for building healthy relationships with one another.

STEP THREE
SHARE POSITIVE
COMMUNICATION

R od, a pharmaceuticals representative in Kansas, and his wife, Sally, a computer programmer, started their marriage with great expectations and happiness. Rod was just starting out in his business. His income was unpredictable, and getting established demanded a great deal of time and energy—both physical and emotional.

"I would sometimes wake up at night," Rod said, "in a cold sweat, feeling anxious about whether I would make it in pharmaceuticals. I worried about having enough money to make ends meet. Some months I made adequate income and some months I didn't. I was an emotional wreck but was too 'macho' to share my feelings with Sally. I wanted her to think I was strong and in control.

"But she wasn't fooled; she's very perceptive. One evening while we were walking in the park, she said, 'Rod, you're pretty uptight about how things are going at work, aren't you?'

"I denied it, but she didn't let me off the hook. 'Yes, you are worried,' she insisted, 'and I think it's natural. But I hate to see you feel that way. Let's talk about this and see if the situation is as bad as it seems and what we can do to make things better.'

"At that point I opened up and shared all of my frustration and insecurity with her. I hadn't talked with anyone about my worries, and it was a great relief to get it all out.

"We talked about ways to cut expenses and things we could do without. Then Sally asked me, 'What would be the worst thing that could possibly happen?' and I answered, 'I would lose my job.' She reminded me that we would still be able to make it on her income and that her job was very stable. We would have to make some changes, but she was confident that we could make it.

"Well, that helped put things in perspective. The situation didn't seem nearly so bad. Then Sally said, 'I think one of the things holding you back in your work has been your worry and anxiety. Why don't you stop worrying about work and start enjoying it?'

"I took her advice, and you know, I began to enjoy my work for the first time. Things improved, and today I am one of the top representatives for the company. But that's not the most important part of the story. The most important part is that on that evening a few years ago, Sally was sensitive enough and loved me enough to know that I was hurting and needed to talk. She cared enough to initiate the conversation. As a result, I felt closer to Sally than I ever had. I think that established our close bond with each other more than any other single event, and it set the pattern for a caring, open communication."

We learn from strong families such as Rod and Sally that communication in its highest sense is a communion of two people—a caring communion.

In the chapter on commitment, we saw that members of strong families *value* each other, but they do something more. They let that valuing—that caring, that commitment—shine through. And when they do, at least two good things happen: They reinforce healthy self-concepts, and they set a climate for continued positive communication.

While *appreciation* (discussed in the last chapter) was the least anticipated characteristic discovered in the research on strong families, the presence of *good communication* patterns was the least surprising. Countless research studies from very diverse fields have revealed effective communication as a factor in building strong families. The strong families in the research for this book verified—in their own words—the formal findings of others.

Strong families spend large amounts of time in conversation. They talk about small, trivial topics as well as the profound, deep issues of life. One mother in Rhode Island made a statement that is typical of our strong families.

We think it is very important to keep in touch with each other and to know where each one is. We want full contact with each other, not 10 or 20 percent contact!

THE VALUE OF COMMUNICATION

When people are asked why communication is so important, they say things such as "Communication is vital to understanding each other" or "Communication keeps you on the same pathway" or "Communication makes you feel loved and vital to the other person."

While these responses are a little vague, they highlight the importance of communication. Maybe looking at what communication *does* for a family will help clarify what communication *is*.

GOOD COMMUNICATION PROMOTES MENTAL HEALTH

Researchers tell us that in extreme cases, people who suffer communication deprivation—such as in solitary confinement—often develop emotional problems, mental disturbances, or psychoses. In less extreme circumstances, people confined to their homes by health problems or difficult circumstances often go deep into themselves. This is not to imply that you cause mental imbalance in your family by not having enough communication, but it is true that you can promote good mental health in family members through frequent, positive communication.

How?

First, just the ability to express thoughts and emotions instead of having to suppress them makes for better mental health. It prevents the building up of anger to the point of bitterness and rage.[1] It gives a way to "vent" and remove power from negative emotions as well as providing a way to share positive emotions.

Second, being able to share ideas and thoughts promotes seeing things from different perspectives and, therefore, encourages positive interaction with others. That type of give-and-take leads to greater success in all aspects of life, as was said long ago in the proverb: "Plans fail for lack of counsel, but with many advisers they succeed."[2] People gain wisdom and balance through communication with others, and when they do, they are more likely to be mentally and emotionally healthy.

Third, the acceptance felt in true, interactive communication gives each family member a good sense of self and self-worth. Each person listens and is listened to. Love is shared in words and in the demonstration of respect and acceptance. The resulting stable sense of self-worth is conducive to mental and emotional health.

Members of strong families have commented on the value of communication to mental health.

Our teenager came home from school very upset. Some girls had teased her because she hasn't begun to blossom physically yet. Fortunately, she was able to talk to me about it. I told her that things were like that when I was a girl too. Our chests are never the right size; girls get teased for too much and too little. She was able, after venting her hurt and anger, to say, "Next time, I'll say..." She has several good retorts planned. We laughed about those. I'm so glad she didn't have to bear that alone.

I get overwhelmed at work; there's always so much to be done and not enough time to do it. I come home and my wife hears me out and gently reminds me of reality again. She gives me perspective and hope.

Last week I had an ugly confrontation with a neighbor. My son and a friend had climbed her dogwood tree. She shooed them away and came over to read me the riot act. I felt she accused me unjustly of being a bad mother who encouraged the kids to ignore other people's property rights. I stewed and fumed until my husband came home. After I told him about it and we talked it through, my bad feelings began to go away. Telling it to him helped me release the anger.

GOOD COMMUNICATION BUILDS BELONGING

No one wants to feel all alone in the world. We all want to feel a part of others; we all want to *belong.*

Remember how despondent Elijah became when he thought he was the only one who stood up for God? He begged, "I have had enough, LORD. Take my life."[3] When God asked him why, he said, "I am the only one left."[4] Feeling all alone is a mixture of terror and despair. It's little surprise that Elijah's loneliness led him to crave death. As part of Elijah's healing and restitution to service, God told him, "I reserve seven thousand in Israel—all whose knees have not bowed down to Baal and all whose mouths have not kissed him."[5] In other words, God said to Elijah, "Don't think you're alone. You're not. You have thousands of brothers and sisters who are like you and want you to be part of them."

Every person needs to know that he or she is a part of a whole; communication is the process through which this sense of belonging is related.

I found in my husband someone with whom I could share my thoughts, ambitions, dreams, and fears. I truly feel that we are two who have become one.

My parents always have time to listen to my problems and concerns. I know they'll have time for me no matter what. They're on my side.

One of the ways that communication helps us feel connected to other people is through the exchange of information. It's hard to feel close to someone you know little about. This exchange of information helps in another way too.

GOOD COMMUNICATION "GREASES THE WHEELS"

Repeatedly, strong families mentioned the importance of communication—even when discussing other characteristics of strong families. Look back through the chapters you've read or glance ahead, and you'll notice how often they say things like "We sat down and *talked* about it" or "We had a *long talk* and decided..." or "We had a family council to *discuss*..."

Strong families face the same problems as everyone else: they overdraw at the bank, the car breaks down, the teenagers sneak beer, grandpa has to come live with them—you name it! The difference is the way they deal with problems. Good communication helps ease daily frustration levels by increasing the family's effectiveness in solving problems.

This means that when the difficulties or trials come, families with good communication find the solution or path to healing.

ARE YOU READY TO MAKE IT HAPPEN?

Positive communication isn't something that *just happens* in good families; these families *make* it happen, as the case of Andrea and Randal illustrates. Randal is an insurance salesman. He and Andrea have been married ten years and have one child.

Selling insurance involves a lot of traveling and a good bit of calling on people at night. If you don't watch it, your family can really get the shaft in this business. You spend so much of your time working and traveling that your family never sees you.

I slid into this pattern. I was out every night during the week, plus I was out of town two weekends each month. I was a stranger to Andrea and the baby.

One day Andrea and I were having lunch together, and I told her I would have to be out of town again that weekend.

She exploded. When she calmed down, she said in her no-nonsense manner, "Randy, do you realize that you have been out every week-night this entire month and there has been only one weekend this month you have been home? We have to do something."

She was right; things had to change. I canceled my weekend travel plans. It was more critical for me to be home.

We talked a long time over the next ten days about alternatives. We made some changes in our lifestyle and communication patterns. One thing I began to do was to call home more often when I traveled. You know, just so we could let each other know how we were doing and what was happening. It's a simple way to say, "Hey, I care about you," and the phone company loves it!

Now when I know I'll be late getting home, I let Andrea know and she takes a nap in the afternoon. Then when I get home, even if it's after midnight, she will be up waiting for me, and we can have a snack together. These times are very special for us. We look forward to them.

If you want to improve your marriage and family like Randal and Andrea did, you can. It takes effort and planning, but it can be done.

Six Rules for Good Communication

Marriage and family therapists not only pinpoint a *lack* of communication as a source of family unhappiness, they also point out that *bad* communication causes unhappiness. To keep that from happening in your family, let's look at some of the things that strong families have learned about good communication. Their experiences help us see how to eliminate faulty ways of communication in favor of effective ones.

Basically, strong families gave six rules for good communication.

RULE #1—ALLOW ENOUGH TIME

A man stood silently with his son, daughter-in-law, and three grandchildren looking over the rim of the Grand Canyon of the Colorado River in Arizona. Instead of being lost in the beauty of the hues and shadows, he found himself thinking about something else altogether. He pondered the evolution of his family—his marriage, the birth of his children, and now being a part of the growth and development of his grandchildren. Finally his thoughts turned to the sight before them, and he marveled at the incredible beauty of this national treasure. He thought of the countless years required to form such a magnificent creation—all of it taking place without a sense of hurry or urgency. He whispered thoughtfully, "Good things take time."

Things of beauty usually do take time: the Grand Canyon, great families, and good communication. Strong families spend time in family communication.

As one father said:

We spend time just talking to each other about all sorts of things. The conversations are usually not about anything profound. Much of what we talk about would be considered trivial by many people, but we enjoy just talking with each other, even if what we're talking about amounts to nothing.

Funny thing is, sometimes we uncover important issues—feelings or values that need to be discussed. And I've always felt that I couldn't expect my wife or child to bring the heavy matters to me if I wasn't interested in the less critical areas of their lives. If my son can't talk with me about cars and tennis, why should he think I'd listen about the drug traffic at school?

While much communication in strong families is spontaneous— "We talk while we do chores together" or "We talk anytime we're together"—some strong families plan a certain time each day for the entire family to be together to talk.

Oteka and Jerry, for example, use dinner as a time for each member of the family to share the most enjoyable experiences of the day. Other families plan special times, such as family night or family councils, for family members to share happy things, problems, and concerns with each other. These families do not shirk talking about difficult or troubling things; but at the same time, they make sure that the positive sides of life are well represented in the dialogues.

One mother noted:

If all we did was focus on problems, I'd go nuts. People who dwell on disaster in their conversations make me wacky. I start drawing circles around my navel. Life is too interesting to be wasted by endless complaining.

So strong families don't spend all their time communicating about problems or worries. They make time to talk about other matters of interest to every family member, both trivial and important.

RULE #2—LISTEN

An Indiana husband said about his wife:

Some people have a hard time believing that my wife is my most trusted advisor. They think you have to be a fount of wisdom to help people, and they don't see Dottie in those terms. But the way my wife helps me isn't by telling me what to do but by listening. She could teach classes on listening! She doesn't interrupt—except maybe to ask a question to clear up a point. She lets me get it all out. So many people don't listen; they're just waiting for you to hush so they can go to talking.

I find that I can take situations of all kinds to Dottie and she'll hear them out. And the amazing thing is, without her offering any advice, I can see things more clearly. Sometimes a solution will come to me as I talk.

The way she listens lets me know she cares about me. She thinks what I have to say is important.

Maybe one of the scriptures that should be embroidered and framed to hang on the wall is James 1:19: "Everyone should be quick to listen, slow to speak and slow to become angry."

Strong family members realize that communication involves two steps: talking and listening. They avoid the trap of focusing on talk to the exclusion of *listen*. In some families, various members can relate to God's frustration with Job when he said, "Listen now, and I will speak."[6] But in strong families, that frustration doesn't exist because each person knows how to listen as well as how to talk. Sometimes they've learned the hard way, as one wife explains:

When we first married, my husband could talk more than anybody. He could go on for hours, it seemed. I'd wait for him to stop so I could say something, and he never would. I'd have to interrupt and say my piece fast to be heard at all. I began to be embarrassed by his monopolizing the conversation when we were with friends.

And frankly, I needed him to respect me enough to listen to me once in a while. It took awhile and some harping, but he saw my side, and with some work, he's learned not to monologue. We used a timer at home to take turns—kind of like you do with children. I'd set it for three minutes and he'd talk; then I'd get the next three—with no unnecessary interruption. As he learned to listen, we put the timer away. We also developed a secret signal to use in public. I'd adjust my left earring to mean he needed to stop talking and listen. Once, he was telling a good story and stopped abruptly in the middle. Then I realized I had reached up to brush my hair back and he had thought I'd sent a signal. We had a good laugh about that one later.

Listening strengthens the relationship between folks by conveying messages of caring and respect. Strong families increase their understanding of each other by being good, active listeners. One mother described what we mean by *active* listening.

My eight-year-old began to complain often of headaches at school. Three times in two weeks the school nurse called because he had come to her office with a headache and wanted to come home. After a while I decided this wasn't a virus, so I questioned him about school. He said everything was fine. His work had been good, so I figured he wasn't having academic problems. I pressed on to recess. I didn't get much, except that Pat had teased him over a missed soccer goal. I continued to ask questions over the next week or so and was careful to note facial expressions and voice tone as well as words. Several times, it came out that Pat had teased, bullied, et cetera. He also had caused the class to lose library time because of his acting out. I began to suspect Pat was a "headache" in more ways than one.

As this mother showed, active listeners notice facial expression, body posture, and voice tone as well as words. They nod or say "okay" or "go on" or something to indicate their attention. And really good listeners "sift," as the nineteenth-century English novelist Dinah Maria Mulock Craik expressed it: "Oh, the comfort, the inexpressible comfort of feeling safe with a person, having neither to weigh thoughts nor measure words, but pouring them all right out, just as they are, chaff and grain together; certain that a faithful hand will take and sift them, keep what is worth keeping, and then with the breath of kindness, blow the rest away."

RULE #3—CHECK IT OUT

Bob had been irritable all evening. He'd snapped at Ann a couple of times over nothing and had been unusually quiet the rest of the time. Of course, Ann was disturbed over this. Naturally, she felt hurt and resentful toward Bob. However, her resentment was based on the assumption that Bob's irritation and negative behavior were directed toward her. As good marriage counselors and good listeners know, this may not be the case at all.

To find out what the problem really was, Ann checked it out.

Checked it out?

Yes. She decided to see if Bob was really angry or upset with her or if something else was going on. She said, "Bob, you've been acting grumpy tonight. Is it because of something that I've done, or is it something else? Do you feel okay?" Bob then shared with Ann that his budget had been cut at work, and because of the cut, he would have to terminate a friend who works in his office. While he hated this turn of events, he had no choice and felt very frustrated. He wasn't upset or angry with Ann at all. If she had not clarified the meaning of his communication, she would have misinterpreted Bob's behavior and may have reacted in a way that would only have made their evening worse.

So as you can see, checking out the meaning of unclear messages is an important technique of good communication. Unclear messages can often be clarified by saying, "I'm not sure I know what you mean by that" or "This is my understanding of what you mean.... Is that correct?"

Vigilance in clarifying fuzzy or distorted messages helps strong families avoid two common communication pitfalls: indirect communication and mind reading.

A New Mexico husband told of his experience with indirect communication:

My wife's family uses a good deal of indirect messages, and they understand each other. My family has always been pretty direct, so you can imagine the interesting misunderstandings Sue and I had until we figured this out. She'd say, "Are there any good movies downtown?" and she'd mean, "I'd like to go to a movie." I would answer the question she voiced by telling her what was playing. Then I'd be surprised when she got angry or sulked. Eventually we figured this pattern out. Now she tries to say, "I'd like to..." instead of hinting, and I'm better about checking to be sure I understand what she really means.

Mind readers, on the other hand, assume they know what others are thinking but don't bother to check it out. James and Debbie talk about how they overcame this habit: "The clearest example was over the issue of visiting my parents," James said. "Debbie hadn't had much of a chance to get to know them before we married, so I assumed she wouldn't want to visit them. I'd fly out to Arizona to visit periodically, but I wouldn't ask her to go."

"Meanwhile," interrupts Debbie, "I jumped to the conclusion that Jim had some dark, ugly reason for not wanting me along. First I thought he was ashamed of me. Then I decided he must have an old girlfriend back home. I'd fret whenever he left but never asked why he didn't want me along."

James continued, "I stupidly assumed that her not asking to go was proof of her lack of interest. Finally my folks came here for my graduation. They enjoyed Debbie so much they said, 'You should come to visit with James.' That caused Debbie and me to discover how dumb our assumptions had been."

RULE #4—GET INSIDE THE OTHER PERSON'S WORLD

We each live in our own unique world. No one sees life exactly the same way you do. The way you look at a certain situation depends on past experiences you have had, the values in which you believe, and your personality characteristics. This means that when two people disagree on an issue, it is not always because one person is right and the other wrong. It is more likely due to the fact that the two people come from different worlds, with different perspectives.

People who are most adept in communication—such as our strong family members—have the ability to get inside another person's world and to see things from that person's point of view. Social scientists call this empathy. Liz, a strong-family member from Tennessee, explained:

Early in our marriage, financial hardship forced us to move close to my in-laws. We didn't have to share a home, but we parked a mobile home on their farm. I soon learned a lot about my parents-in-law, but more important, I learned a lot about my husband from them.

Let me give you some for-instances. I had been disturbed by what I saw as Hank's habit of arguing—especially when I'd try to discuss something at meals. In my home, mealtime was a time for pleasant talk about ideas or events. But it seemed that Hank and I would always wind up in a disagreement when we sat down to eat. I began to worry that we weren't compatible. Then I observed—over a period of months—that he and his folks like lively conversations, and it isn't uncommon for one of them to play devil's advocate just to keep things interesting. They don't get emotionally involved; no one gets angry or hurt. That is what clued me in that these weren't real arguments. They're more like debates.

Another area of misunderstanding cleared up when I noted how Hank's mom keeps house. He and I had fought over housekeeping—I'd fuss that our place was messy; he'd say it was comfortable. When I got it cleaned to suit me, he felt it was too sterile. One day it dawned on me that Hank's folks are more relaxed about housekeeping. They're clean—don't get me wrong—but they like to have books and magazines handy. She always has needlework materials out—on the table or scattered about the living room. And we do have taste differences in decorating. I prefer simple, uncluttered designs, neutral colors, few decorations. Hank grew up with wallpaper designs, ornate furniture, and much more bric-a-brac. We've compromised on this one. And that compromise was made easier by understanding each other's point of view.

RULE #5—KEEP THE MONSTERS IN LATE-NIGHT MOVIES

Remember when you were a kid and you played the monster game with your friends? Someone would yell, "Here comes the green monster." Everybody would scream and howl and run amok. The monster game was scary but fun.

Adults also play a "here comes the green monster" game, but the adult version isn't much fun. It creates anxiety, destroys good communication, and ruins relationships.

Strong families have learned to keep several communication monsters under lock and key: *criticizing, evaluating,* and *acting superior.* Their comments provide some insights.

Mike *never attacks me personally when we fight.*

You *know, parents spend an awful lot of time fussing at their children, pointing out what they do wrong, and telling them they need to improve here or there. It can get to the point where children feel they are not pleasing their parents—that they're bad in some way. We try to point out what our children do right every chance we get.*

I *have an aunt who comes to visit about once a year. She's a dear woman and has many good qualities, but she always makes me feel as if I am being measured. She isn't openly critical, but I can tell she's comparing my job, my housekeeping, my children, my life to what someone else has and does. I don't guess she realizes how much she threatens my self-esteem. I'm glad we're not like that in our marriage or with our kids. I'd never want my husband or my children to feel about me like I feel about my aunt.*

I'd like to brag about my wife just a little; she has such a wonderful attitude and manner. I haven't met very many people who are more intelligent than she is. She's a physician—very respected in our community—and it would be easy for her to feel just a notch or two above ordinary folks, but she doesn't. I'm sure there are people who wonder what it's like to live with her. I can tell you she never makes me feel defensive or inferior. I always feel she has genuine esteem for me.

In his book *Love Busters*, Dr. Willard Harley refers to these "monsters" of criticizing, evaluating, and acting superior as "disrespectful judgment." His experience heading twenty-three mental health clinics verifies the research behind this book. When disrespectful judgment takes place, relationships will fail. Strong families banish such "love busters" and don't allow them to destroy all the good that they've accomplished in their homes.

The following scripture sums this up nicely: "Do not let any unwholesome talk come out of your mouths, but only what is helpful for building others up according to their needs, that it may benefit those who listen."[7]

RULE #6—KEEP IT HONEST

The communication patterns in strong families are characterized by honesty and openness. People say what they mean and mean what they say.

That doesn't surprise us because this is exactly what God commands us to do. "Each of you must put off falsehood and speak truthfully to his neighbor, for we are all members of one body."[8]

But honesty is more than not lying; it is an absence of manipulation. Our strong families felt strongly about not manipulating or being manipulated.

It makes me angry to see a couple at a party in one of those situations where you know they disagree and he will argue his case and end by saying, "Isn't that right, dear?" What can she say? That makes me very uncomfortable. Thank goodness my husband and I don't do that to each other!

We became aware this summer of a bad habit our daughter had picked up. She was exaggerating her weaknesses (for lack of a better word) in order to get people to do things for her. I think it began when she broke her ankle and discovered how nice it was to be waited on. Then we noticed she was "no good at math," so big brother was helping her by figuring her paper route bills. Or her ankle "hurt too much" to help with chores. Or she "had a headache" and couldn't go somewhere with us. We were able to correct her tactics by refusing to do things she could do herself.

My husband used to bully people in order to get his way. He would yell at salespeople, shout, or storm off from me. I knew early in our relationship that he wasn't truly mean; he barked a lot but didn't bite. After a while I tired of feeling pushed around. A counselor helped us identify and correct the problem.

Members of strong families don't resort to bullying, outwitting, blaming, dominating, or controlling. They don't play on dependency; they aren't silent, long-suffering martyrs who create guilt. All those methods of manipulating others lead to dishonesty and shallowness in relationships.

But some folks use "honesty" as an excuse to be exceedingly unkind. Strong families maintain a balance of honesty and kindness. They aren't apt to let Sis go out in a dress and hairdo that look ridiculous just because they don't want to offend her. On the other hand, they won't use one mistake in her judgment as an excuse to blast her taste, time management, hygiene, and study habits.

The important principle is the idea that any disagreement, any thought, any aspect of human relationships can be expressed in a positive, nonjudgmental, nonhurtful way. God said it like this: "Speaking the truth in love, we will in all things grow up into him who is the Head, that is, Christ."[9]

Even disputes over how the toothpaste is squeezed can be handled with love and gentleness and kindness.

Fred, for example, has been exasperated by his teenaged daughters who haven't caught on to "the right way" to squeeze toothpaste. "From the bottom, of course," he chuckled. But rather than make it into a big, angry issue, he had some fun with his daughters. He kidnapped the toothpaste and left this note in the medicine cabinet:

Dear Teenaged Daughters:

The tartar-control toothpaste has been kidnapped and is being held for ransom.

It will be returned when my daughters, Ellen and Andrea, pledge to treat it kindly and gently and not to squirt blue goo through the stupid pop-top that I hate and leave it all messy.

Signed,
The Silverback

The Silverback signature was a reference to Fred's nickname. As a middle-aged male, he has so much hair on his back that his daughters took to calling him "Silverback" in reference to the dominant male gorilla in the movie *Gorillas in the Mist*. "We have a running family joke about my hairiness. The girls want to pay for a complete wax all over my body as a Christmas present."

Anyway, Fred got his point across about toothpaste with a bit of good fun and humor. Did this ploy work? "Nah. Not perfectly. But I've got a new strategy I'm planning right now."

The comments of a Georgia husband illustrate the need to give kindness as well as take it:

I depend on my family for support and understanding. It is a tremendous comfort to be able to dump frustrations and anger on the sympathetic ears at home. I also realize that I can't just be the "dumper" all the time; sometimes I have to be the sympathetic ear.

Kindness is more than reserving harsh or hurtful words. Sometimes it is seeing to the needs of the rest of the family before you expect them to help you with your own.

And it means using considerate words. An Ohio mother said:

We practice our manners at home too. "Please" and "thank you" are as important there as at school or work. If one of us is going to be late, we let the family know; it's just common courtesy. It would be stupid not to be as considerate and as pleasant to family as we are to strangers.

WHEN CONFLICT ARISES

Without fail, whenever we talk about strong families, someone asks if they ever argue. Yes they do! And there are good reasons why. Jake, a retired tailor with a good measure of wisdom, put it this way: "If you didn't care about somebody, you wouldn't get mad!" For example, a wife might get angry with her husband for driving too fast because she doesn't want him to get killed.

Another reason for conflict in strong families has already been mentioned: They are *real* people in a *real* world. They disagree with each other; they make mistakes; they get fatigued and stressed; problems arise. Again, it is not the lack of conflict that sets strong families apart; it's the way they deal with it: When conflict arises, they are creative and caring.

Researchers who specialize in analyzing the nuts and bolts of family communication like to watch families in their natural environment—in the living room, in the kitchen, at the dining-room table—and they have identified four ways that families resolve conflicts.

1. I WIN, YOU LOSE; OR YOU WIN, I LOSE

In this method of "resolving conflict," someone in the family pulls rank on the others, overpowers them, and wins the argument. This is basically a "because-I'm-bigger-than-you" or "because-I'm-your-mother" approach. Most family therapists would see this, generally, as a mistake. While every family on earth probably adopts this approach on occasion, some families don't know any other style. But the problem is that hardly anybody loves the boss. They may *respect* the boss, which usually translates "fear," but they don't generally *like* the boss much. Family members in this type of situation tend to engage in a long-term guerrilla warfare against the person who tries to overpower everyone else. They go underground and become masters at subterfuge: lying, cheating, ignoring, weaseling. They may not be totally pleased with their own manipulative behaviors, but they see them as necessary in the face of injustice.

Of course, while the Bible teaches us to respect authority, Jesus made it clear that the best kind of leader is one who is also a servant. Since parents are leaders, his teaching applies here. He said,

> You know that those who are regarded as rulers of the Gentiles lord it over them, and their high officials exercise authority over them. Not so with you. Instead, whoever wants to become great among you must be your servant, and whoever wants to be first must be slave of all. For even the Son of Man did not come to be served, but to serve, and to give his life as a ransom for many.[10]

The "I win, you lose; or you win, I lose" way of handling conflict isn't the best way, and it usually isn't a godly way.

2. ONE PERSON WITHDRAWS

Withdrawal is another common, problematic way of solving family conflict. Somebody backs off, basically saying, "I quit. I'm not going to play this game anymore." Sometimes people use the silent treatment, refusing to talk to the other party. One family therapist described a family he had worked with: "The wife got so mad that she refused to speak to her husband for a long time."

"How long is 'long'?" you might ask.

"Over two years. The tension in the family was indescribable when they finally came in for therapy."

That's astounding! That may be the record time for the silent treatment. Perhaps Guinness has registered a longer time, but whatever the record, the silent treatment is not recommended by any credible family researcher or therapist. It just tends to make matters in a family even worse.

And it completely ignores God's command to deal with the anger one feels that very day, before the sun goes down.

3. STANDOFF

This approach basically says that the disputants have agreed to disagree. They cannot come to any consensus; there is no compromise in sight. It would be ideal if human beings could get along together perfectly, but we all live in a less-than-ideal world. Strong families have strong family members: strong moms, strong dads, strong kids. Spouses believe it is important that each be free to believe as she or he chooses, and parents believe it is important for their children to have opinions and the courage to stick to their opinions when need be. Therefore, there may be some issues in strong families that will not be easily resolved. A group consensus will not develop. This is not necessarily a sign of a problem in the family; rather, it can be interpreted as a strength. It can be seen as the family's respect for individual freedom.

Please don't misinterpret what's being said here. Parents must have certain power over their children if they are to do their job as good, loving, and capable parents. A parent knows more about life than a child and has to exercise her or his authority.

It's easy to go off the deep end on both sides of this issue. Sometimes parents withdraw from children so fully that they do not exercise any control over them. This, in extreme cases, becomes child neglect, pure and simple. On the other hand, some parents are so controlling, so power-hungry, that they make life miserable for their children, stifling them. This controlling behavior can also become abusive if carried to the extreme. The answer lies somewhere in the middle: The parent needs to take the child's feelings and concerns into careful consideration but also must have the courage and strength to make the final decision.

4. COMPROMISE OR CONSENSUS

The classic, positive approach to conflict resolution recommended by most professionals is that people learn how to split the difference in a conflict or work together to come to a reasonable agreement that benefits everyone. This is the ideal approach, and strong families do this regularly.

SIX TACTICS FOR HANDLING CONFLICTS CORRECTLY

Following are six tactics that strong families use to handle conflict with *compromise* or *consensus*.

TACTIC #1—DEAL WITH CONFLICTS QUICKLY

One tactic that strong families use in disagreements is to air grievances while they are current. They don't hoard complaints to use as weapons. Jack and his wife are typical of the strong families in this respect.

We cannot stand to have contention between us. It bothers both of us to be at odds with each other. As a result, we deal with sore spots as quickly as possible. Sometimes we have to wait awhile—say until we get home from work or until we calm down a bit. But we deal with them as soon as possible rather than letting them get bigger overnight.

Jack obviously practices what God said about this: "Do not let the sun go down while you are still angry."[11]

TACTIC #2—DEAL WITH ONE ISSUE AT A TIME

A benefit of dealing with problems as they arise is that the families are more apt to be dealing with *one problem at a time*. Paula, from Virginia, provides some ideas about why this is a good rule to follow.

After several hair-curling arguments that started with the overextended budget and went to dirty socks stuffed under the bed to hair in the sink to both sets of in-laws to where to vacation, we wised up. How could anybody sort out all those things? If we could put socks, hair, in-laws, and vacations on hold, we could concentrate on the budget. We could handle one problem; that's manageable. Five problems at once are overwhelming.

TACTIC #3—BE SPECIFIC

For a long time I was angry at my wife because I thought she was spending money too freely. I'd complain that she was spending too much. She'd say she couldn't cut corners any more than she was.

Finally, during one fight, she said, "Just tell me how to spend less."

"Well," I said, "you do a good job on groceries, and you don't splurge on gifts or things for yourself—but you could spend a lot less on clothes for the children."

Suddenly it hit me: That's what was really bothering me. She suggested that she could choose less expensive shops for the kids' clothes—especially playclothes.

It was rather funny. When I could narrow it down to my specific gripe, she and I could deal with it.

Strong-family members have a greater track record of successes in solving problems because a specific complaint is easier to treat. "You never talk to me" is harder to manage than "I wish we could have thirty minutes each evening without TV, the paper, or the kids."

TACTIC #4—BECOME ALLIES

Probably the approach of strong families that spares them the most grief in conflict situations is that of attacking the problem rather than each other. One spouse said,

It would be silly to get caught up in personal attacks when we fight. All that does is hurt feelings and fan the fires. We try to see ourselves as being on the same side—as a team. The enemy is the problem. We're fighting it—not each other.

TACTIC #5—BAN THE BOMBS

A spouse or children can be devastated in innumerable ways. We think of these implements of destruction as "atomic bombs." They're the weapons you hold on to for that last-ditch effort. Usually you're going down fast or are consumed by anger, and so you vent all your wrath.

Members of strong families have declared a freeze on such nuclear weapons. One Alabama wife said:

I know more about my husband and children than anyone else does. I know their fears, their vulnerabilities. I have power to hurt them.

So why don't I pull out all the stops and say those dreadful things that would allow me to "win"? Because that is too high a price to pay for winning the battle. Generals make that mistake sometimes. My son is a World War II buff, and I've heard him remark several times, "So-and-so won this battle, but the casualties were terribly high. They won, but it cost too much."

I feel that it would be a serious violation of the trust we have in each other to use our knowledge, or closeness, as weapons. Even when I get very angry, I keep sight of that. To use sensitive areas as attack points is a good way to destroy a marriage or parent-child relationship.

TACTIC #6—OPEN UP UNDERSTANDING

Strong families put many of their communication skills to work when conflicts surface. They check to be sure they understand what a spouse or child is saying; they actively listen to feelings as well as words. Sound familiar? Those general communication skills were listed earlier in this chapter. Now let's see how they work in handling conflict.

One husband described a battle that failed to materialize because he and his wife checked out their understanding.

I had been planning to send some money to my parents to help them through a tight spot. They're retired and had had some major expenses: Dad had surgery, and a windstorm blew a tree onto the roof. Anyway, I had the check ready to mail when Cindy objected.

I could feel my temperature rising but asked, "Why don't you want me to mail this?" She said, "I want you to send it; I'm not objecting to that. I just want you to wait about three days until a paycheck can be deposited to cover it."

By controlling myself enough to be sure I understood what she meant, we avoided a heated argument. If I'd jumped on her for interfering, being stingy, hating my folks, et cetera—well, what a waste of energy!

Part of developing understanding involves keying in on feelings. One woman came close to being profound when she said, "Feelings are real, but they aren't always logical." She went on to say:

My *daughter complained that we're too strict on her. She said she felt confined and not trusted. When we looked at the situation, we saw that our rules weren't overly strict, and we couldn't find any evidence of not trusting her. She admitted as much herself. Yet she still felt confined.*

When we thought together a bit more, it became clear that she was anxious to be involved in several activities that require driving. She was impatient to grow up.

I've discovered that the best thing to do in situations like this is just to acknowledge her feelings. "Yes, I understand that you feel restricted. Perhaps this is why you feel this way…but I really believe these feelings will pass. We might do this or that to help."

THE LIFEBLOOD

While strong families have their share of conflict, they know how to deal with it effectively, and the conflicts become an opportunity for growth. Because strong families have developed positive communication habits, their disagreements are problem-solving sessions rather than brawls.

And their good communication patterns do more than smooth the conflict; they sustain mental health and nurture intimacy. Effective communication ensures that the commitment they have and the appreciation and affection they feel are expressed. Communication truly is the lifeblood of strong relationships.

FAMILY AT WORK

Putting It to Work—Six Ideas for Your Family

1. *Set aside some time each day to talk with your spouse* (fifteen to thirty minutes). Nick and Nancy Stinnett like to get up early enough to have coffee and conversation before the workday begins. Pick the time and situation best for you and then *block that time* for each other. Make it as concrete as any appointment in your life.

2. *Take an objective look at your communication habits.* Are you guilty of monologue, mind reading, indirect messages? Most of us are to some extent. Pick one bad habit to correct. Focus on it for one month. Work on another next month.

3. *Designate a mealtime as a time for sharing.* Plan for the whole family to be together; share your most interesting events of the day at dinner or plans for the day at breakfast. Avoid disciplining the children or raising inflammatory issues at mealtime. Keep the mood pleasant. John and Nikki DeFrain regularly have dinner with their two daughters who are still at home. Sometimes that means eating at 5:00 P.M., other times at 6:30, but they feel it's well worth the schedule juggling to keep in touch with day-to-day happenings in each others' lives.

4. *Establish rituals and traditions.* This is an excellent way for family members to stay in contact with each other. Your family probably already has some traditions. Maybe you'd like to start some others. Following are a few ideas to get you started:

   ◆ Hugs for everyone at bedtime
   ◆ Games and popcorn on Saturday nights
   ◆ A canoe trip or whitewater rafting each June
   ◆ Egg hunts at Easter (Use plastic eggs, and instead of money or candy, insert slips of paper redeemable for treats: lunch with Mom, a day at the beach or museum with both parents, or a weekend bike ride with Dad.)
   ◆ Special stories at Christmas, Memorial Day, Easter, Halloween, Valentine's Day, July 4, or other events (Harry and Jody Heath enjoyed reading *Miracle on 34th Street* for many Christmas seasons. They read it aloud to their children and, in time, their grandchildren.)
   ◆ A barbecue and fireworks each July 4 or Labor Day
   ◆ A weekend at a luxury hotel each anniversary (Leave the kids with grandparents.)
   ◆ Flowers for special occasions (One family member had a wonderful way of honoring her parents. Each year on her birthday

she would send her parents flowers and a card saying how much she loved them and thanking them for being such good parents.)

- ◆ A stroll through last year's calendar each New Year's Eve (Get the family together and go through the calendar month by month, remembering special events and family happenings. You'll be surprised at how similar your calendar is to a diary and how much communication it will stimulate.)

5. *Keep a family diary or journal.* As you go about your daily life, write down funny stories or heartwarming incidents that happen in your family. You may even wish to chronicle the sad events such as the death of family members. It could be anything from a phrase your two-year-old says to a recounting of an evening's somewhat bizarre occurrences. Rolf Olsen, a freelance writer from Tulsa, wrote and told us about a special family journal he and his family have just begun. So far, it includes written entries, a couple of drawings, and printed programs from one daughter's piano recital. Photos will be added soon. The journal begins:

> May 1, 1999—
>
> [Daughter Anna] I got our family's first chiggers.
>
> [Dad] We reached an agreement to buy forty acres with a house, a pond, a tractor, and a horse.

Dad thinks that Anna regards chigger bites as a badge of honor. Certainly the family journal will be a treasure to them all.

6. *On birthdays, videotape the birthday child.* On the videotape, have the birthday child respond to a list of questions one or both parents have put together. These questions can include the child's likes and dislikes of foods, chores, or school subjects. You might have the child talk about a current hobby, sport, collection, or pet. Have the child wear a favorite outfit and sing a song or read a story she's written or explain a drawing he's done. Everyone will enjoy reviewing these tapes from previous years, and your family will have an invaluable keepsake.

STEP FOUR
SPEND TIME TOGETHER

The ice storm had made travel perilous and virtually impossible. Normal activities were halted for three days. Schools—even the university—were closed. Many businesses had shut down. Some were frustrated by the inconvenience and interruption of their daily routine. Not eight-year-old Elizabeth! She was delighted.

She had both of her parents at home. They couldn't go to work or run errands. So they kept a warm fire going in the fireplace. They read stories and played games. They explored the ice-coated world outside. They had popcorn and hot chocolate—"as much as we wanted." As the ice thawed and the three-day freeze was coming to an end, Elizabeth said to her parents, "These have been the best days of my life."

What an important message from the heart of this child. It fits nicely with a comment by eleven-year-old Raoul, "I wish everybody would pay more attention to kids. That's something we really need. Sometimes grownups pay attention, but not a lot. They're kind of all wrapped up in their jobs, and they don't really pay attention to little children."[1]

In surveys where children are asked, "What do you think makes a happy family?" they often surprise us with their wisdom. Their most common response is not money, cars, fine homes, or televisions. The answer they give most frequently is *doing things together*—the very reason that Elizabeth said to her parents that the three days of the ice storm were the best days of her life.

JOURNEY OF HAPPY MEMORIES

How would you like to take a brief journey—a journey of happy memories? Are you game? Okay, here's how it works: Sit down in a favorite chair and get comfortable. Take your shoes off; close your eyes. Relax. Think back. Way back to when you were a kid. What are the happiest memories of your family life during your childhood? Run through your mental videotapes until you come to the best one of all. Now focus on this one time.... What's happening? Who's there? What's going on? What do you see? Smell? Hear? Taste? Feel? Why is it so great? If you really participate, you'll probably end up sitting there with your eyes shut and a big grin on your face, smiling about a happy memory from long, long ago.

Through interviews and questionnaires, many strong families took the same journey you just did. Following are some very common examples of what they remembered.

I remember stories Mom and Dad told me when they tucked me in bed.

Going with Dad to work on the farm. I felt so important. So superior, because my little brother wasn't big enough to go. Every few weeks, Dad and I would scoop out the pig barn, and we'd talk and talk. It was great.

Having the whole family together at Christmas was special. All the grandpas and grandmas and aunts and uncles and thousands of kids. They made us kids eat in the kitchen together. I thought it was so neat then, but it must have been pandemonium.

Singing together. Yes, singing. We had an old piano, and I learned to play, and we would all sing corny songs.

Vacation. We would go fifty miles to the lake and rent a cabin. A cheap cabin. And Dad would swim with us and dunk me.

My dad and I would cook Sunday lunch together. We were all too busy during the week to take much time, but Sundays, Dad and I would make something special like hamburgers or bean sandwiches.

Mom and I would scrub the kitchen floor every Saturday morning. I was about ten or twelve. We would talk "girl-talk" and giggle and tease. Sometimes we'd have a water fight, and everyone in the family would come into the kitchen, and we'd be rolling around on the floor, wet and wriggly with soapsuds in our hair. What a mom!

Now that you've read other people's stories about their best childhood memories and considered your own, you'll notice at least two important things: First, years and years later, the times we adults remember about our childhood, those happiest memories, are times spent with our loved ones—simply doing things together.

Second, you will find that our best memories of childhood rarely have anything to do with money. In American society we are bombarded by messages telling us to spend, spend, spend and consume, consume, consume. And yet, when, for this research, thousands of people were asked to tell about their happiest childhood memories, hardly anyone told a story about something that cost the family a lot of money. Sometimes they were on vacation together, but often they were camping out or staying at a budget motel. Sometimes they were at a movie, but not very often. Only rarely, out of thousands of stories, did anyone ever say that their best memory came from their visit to some expensive theme park or vacation "paradise" hundreds of miles from home. And only once did someone describe a super memory of their family eating a fancy meal together in an expensive restaurant.

MAKE TIME TO MAKE MEMORIES

Those two seemingly universal truths—that our fondest memories are of what we do with our families and that money isn't the key to those memories—find support in the wisdom of Solomon. In his beautiful poetry we call Ecclesiastes, Solomon talked of the importance of time and how conflicting things in our lives take their turns requiring our time. Remember these haunting words?

There is a time for everything,
> and a season for every activity under heaven:
> a time to be born and a time to die,
> a time to plant and a time to uproot,
> a time to kill and a time to heal,
> a time to tear down and a time to build,
> a time to weep and a time to laugh,
> a time to mourn and a time to dance,
> a time to scatter stones and a time to gather them,
> a time to embrace and a time to refrain,
> a time to search and a time to give up,
> a time to keep and a time to throw away,
> a time to tear and a time to mend,
> a time to be silent and a time to speak,
> a time to love and a time to hate,
> a time for war and a time for peace.[2]

If you've ever slowly read Ecclesiastes, hearing the lament of an aging man who had decided that all of life is "meaningless, meaningless," you know that Solomon's view of time is that most of us waste it. We pursue the wrong things and forget to enjoy what is really important. Solomon tried pleasure, riches, fame, sex, and all the other pursuits common to mankind. He finally came to the conclusion—after living his own sordid life and observing the lives of thousands of others—that we should live our lives simply, concentrating on those things that are truly important. As he neared the end of his life, he bemoaned the meaninglessness of most lives, while giving grudging admiration to those who got it right. Among those he observed as having lived well are those who:

- Find satisfaction in simple pleasures, such as food and their work.[3]
- Aren't alone in this world but have others who can give them help, warmth, and defense against outside forces.[4]

- Can sleep sweetly without worries and anxieties.[5]
- Can enjoy their children and the blessings of their lives.[6]

Solomon is right, you know. The people who concentrate on the simple, important things of life are much happier. If you participated in the "journey of happy memories" from the previous section, compare what you felt as you relived those memories with what you feel in the hectic rat race of typical modern life.

Now, think what memories you are creating for your children by the lifestyle you currently live. What will they remember years from now if asked to think back on happy childhood memories? Are you honestly helping to create those memories for them, or is your own misdirection of life denying them that needed root of happiness?

Neither money, fame, prestige, large houses, new cars, fancy schools, nor any of a whole list of things some people sacrifice their families for will create your children's happiest childhood memories. Being with loved ones is the key, and this is an important thing for all of us to know. We waste precious time and energy scrambling for money, thinking it can buy happiness.

It can't.

Seeking it too intensely just leads to bad things. "For the love of money is a root of all kinds of evil. Some people, eager for money, have wandered from the faith and pierced themselves with many griefs."[7] Please don't let yourself reach the end of your life with the "grief" that you didn't spend the time with your family that you should have—and that you really want to.

Don't misunderstand. The intent here is not to convince you to take a vow of poverty—the strong-families research didn't reveal that living in poverty brought happy childhood memories. But neither did the many studies conducted show any meaningful connection between money and family happiness or family strengths. The strong families studied come from all social classes: low income, middle income, and high income. The interviews revealed thriving low-income families and miserable high-income families.

The truly moving and memorable times in one's life as a child are not bought and sold. That should come as important news to parents striving to make ends meet. Give the kids yourself. That's more important than things. They will remember *you*.

If you're there for them.

BENEFITS OF SHARED FAMILY TIME

Spending time together as a family reaps other benefits in addition to creating happy memories.

IT LEADS TO GOOD COMMUNICATION

Strong families realize that communication isn't going to be good unless they spend time together. One North Dakota father said,

My wife understands all our two-year-old's jabber because the two of them spend lots of time together. Margaret was there when little Lyn named rabbits "raboos." Lyn calls alligators "cup" because she has a drinking cup with an alligator on it. It makes sense when you know the details. It's like that in other areas of communication. You have to spend time with people to know them and to talk with them to get beyond superficial matters. Some families I know aren't face-to-face long enough each week to discuss football scores and the weather much less get on to matters of heart and mind.

IT'S AN ANTIDOTE TO ISOLATION, LONELINESS, AND ALIENATION

A recent newspaper story reported findings from a study of the lives and backgrounds of several modern assassins. The investigators identified a number of shared characteristics, including isolation, loneliness, and a feeling of being apart from the rest of the world.

Why tell you that? Because it boldly underscores one of the benefits of shared family time: It is an antidote to isolation, loneliness, and alienation. If feeling isolated and alone can contribute to *murder*, just think what feeling accepted and loved can lead to. Comments from strong families tell how much benefit comes from the good feelings developed in shared family times. Family members in strong families know they are liked and wanted; they know they'll never be abandoned.

A mother from Maine noted:

We spend time together because we like each other. It isn't like "This is a good thing to do, so we'd better plan time together." We enjoy each other's company. Frankly, I get lonesome for my husband and kids when we're apart for very long.

A New York father said:

I had a disturbing experience when I was forty-three years old. I lost a battle with a hepatitis bug and was confined at home for several months to recuperate. My colleagues at work called to inquire about me at first and then drifted away. Except for two close friends and my family, everyone else forgot about my difficulties in a hurry. I don't blame them, and I'm not bitter or complaining. I've been guilty of the same thing myself. What the experience did was make me realize which people are truly important to me. I'm really fortunate to have a wife and daughters, a mother (my father is dead), a brother, in-laws, and a few close friends who care. Spending time with these folks isn't a luxury; it's a necessity. They save me from being lost and alone.

IT PROVIDES A FAMILY IDENTITY

A third benefit of spending time together is that the family develops its own identity—a group unity and a sense of their place in history. Strong family members talked about family identity in these ways:

An Oklahoma woman said,

I remember visiting my Ohio grandmother, aunts, uncles, and cousins each summer. Without fail, the adults would comment on how much my sister and I had grown and would add, "They sure have the Johnson eyes and hair." Dark brown, almost black, eyes and dark brown hair do run in the family. Hearing that summer after summer reinforced the feeling that I was connected to these people, even though I only saw them once a year.

An Ohio man said,

Photographs are very important to us. We have albums and albums full, plus a huge box of them that need to be put into albums. All the important events in our family have been recorded—our wedding, the births and growth of the children, vacations, first days of school, new cars and houses, pets, and on it goes. The kids love to look at the pictures and see what they looked like as babies; our seventeen-year-old looks remarkably like her mother's wedding photo—when she was twenty.

In this part of the country, tornadoes occasionally wipe houses completely out. I've thought that if that ever happened to us, the material thing I would miss the most would be our family photographs.

IT NURTURES RELATIONSHIPS

Hostility and violence are elements in about one-third of the divorces in this country. And certainly, many unhappy families are plagued with anger and strong emotions. But many therapists feel that most family dissatisfaction and dissolution revolve around a lack of emotion. The spouses don't hate each other; they feel no great anger. But they don't love or care for each other either. The relationships simply fizzle and die.

Over and over strong families have said that relationships must be nurtured—like a plant or a baby. Otherwise, they fail to grow. In their time together, good families nurture relationships. Their comments increase our understanding.

We spend as much time working together as playing. There are always dishes to wash, laundry to fold, grass to mow, leaves to rake. But that isn't bad by any means. We have had some of our best, closest times working together.

We've just spent a couple of weeks at my folks' home, and one of the joys of the visit has been watching our toddler and his grandparents together. Granddad has read bunches of books to him. Danny brings them and dumps the books in Granddad's lap and crawls up. Naturally, Dad drops whatever else he's doing to read to Danny.

Danny and Grandma go out for special walks. They hunt lizards or crickets or roly-poly bugs; they smell flowers and watch birds; they wade in the puddles left by the rain. Grandma has a cache of M & Ms that she and Danny keep as their secret. I'd be pressed to say who has the most fun.

I am thankful for the time they're having together. Mom and Dad are thoroughly enjoying it, and Danny's life is definitely enriched.

My *husband and I like to sneak away about twice a year all by ourselves. Chicago is a favorite place to go for our escape weekends. It's close enough that we can drive there in a couple of hours, and there's always something—a museum exhibit, theater, or show—to do. We need those times to concentrate on each other. We dress up and put on our best manners. We flirt with each other. Maybe that sounds silly, but it makes us feel more like we did when we were dating. In a sexy dress and perfume, holding hands over a French dinner by candlelight, I feel different than in jeans at McDonald's wrestling the kids.*

THE NATURE OF TIME TOGETHER

If you are ready to reassess your priorities and exchange the seemingly important things for the truly important matter of spending family time together, we need first to look at the nature of togetherness in strong families. Misunderstanding and misinterpretation are easy in a couple of areas. As you plan your time, understand the nature of that time.

BOTH QUALITY AND QUANTITY

Several years ago, someone suggested that the *quality* of the time spent with family is what's most important. As a result, a debate started over whether *quality* or *quantity* determines the value of time spent with loved ones. Members of strong families have resolved the debate. A working mother from Wisconsin said,

I firmly believe women should not immerse themselves in family to the exclusion of everything else. But to excuse myself from spending time with my daughters by saying, "It was only fifteen minutes, but it was high quality," is a cop-out, pure and plain.

An Arkansas man agreed.

My wife and I took one of those weekend marriage-enrichment seminars. Two questions really hit us hard. The leader asked us to estimate how many minutes we spent in taking out the garbage each week. We didn't know what was coming, so we answered truthfully: "About five minutes a day or thirty-five minutes a week." Then she asked, "How many minutes a day do you and your spouse spend in conversation?" You guessed it! The garbage got more time! We're fooling ourselves if we think that five minutes a day is enough time to maintain a marriage. And it certainly isn't enough to make the marriage grow.

George Rekers, a family therapist, uses a story about a steak to clarify the relationship between quality and quantity. He asks that you imagine you've gone to a new gourmet restaurant and that you decide to treat yourself to their best steak, even though it costs twenty-eight dollars. The steak arrives on an expensive china plate, served with flair by an impeccably dressed waiter. But you note with shock and dismay that the steak is a one-inch cube. In horror, you question the waiter, who assures you that quality is what counts and this steak is *the best*. But if you're very hungry, you know that quantity also counts.

Strong families realize that quantity and quality go hand in hand. The time they spend together needs to be good time—no one enjoys hours of bickering, arguing, pouting, or bullying—but the time also needs to be of sufficient quantity—quality interaction just isn't likely to develop in a few minutes.

ABUNDANT BUT NOT STIFLING

Our strong families work, play, attend church, vacation, and regularly eat meals together. Yet their togetherness is not smothering, for it has boundaries. Individuals are not swallowed up and lost in the group.

The balance between too much and not enough individualism is critical. Families are destroyed when they go to either of two extremes. They go to an extreme on one end if they allow the world and its cares and seductions to draw them apart. They go to the opposite extreme if they become so fixated on each other that they lose their individual identities in the process. Strong families said this in other ways.

My wife goes out every Thursday night to gardening class. This is not my cup of tea. So I enjoy the time with the kids, and when my wife comes in at 11:00 P.M., she is full of enthusiasm and good stories. She is refreshed, and Fridays are better for it.

I have a very busy, very satisfying career at the university. The danger for me and my husband is not that I'll lose my identity (or that he'll lose his), but that we'll grow apart. If I'm not careful, my life could fill up and squeeze him out. So we are sure to spend time together each day. We're especially fond of walks in the evening. Away from phones and interruptions, we share what has happened, make plans, and stay in touch.

A Minnesota mother mentioned another important way the togetherness in strong families is kept from smothering the individuals.

We do many things as a family, but not everyone participates in every activity. Being together may mean that my daughter and I go shopping or my son and I go to his karate class or both kids and I go to the library. My husband and I spend time without the kids; the kids do things together. It's a mix-up of twos or threes as often as it is all four of us together. Sooner or later, we each spend time with everyone else in the family. And those one-on-one relationships—mother-daughter, father-daughter, mother-son, father-son, husband-wife, brother-sister—have a chance to develop too.

PLANNED BUT NOT MECHANICAL

One of the realities of modern life is that many activities and people compete for our attention and time. Almost everyone has a drawer full of projects to finish—"someday when I have a little free time." Strong families are not exempted from the shortage of time, but they have learned some valuable truths.

We discovered fairly soon in our parenting years that family times don't just happen. They have to be planned. If we don't watch out, we end up scattered all over the town—Carl working at his office; me at bridge, League of Women Voters, or PTA; the kids at band practice, basketball, or a friend's house.

Our church encourages families to set aside one night each week as family night. No one plans outside activities or has friends over to visit on that night. We have ours on Mondays. We do different things. In the summer, we may cook out and play yard games. Sometimes we work on a project like setting up our aquarium. In the winter, we gather around the fireplace to pop popcorn or toast nuts and to read mystery stories aloud.

We try to do a variety of things so that family night doesn't get to be routine and dull. And of course, we spend other time together too. You can't just designate Monday as family time and let it go at that. That's like taking a bath only on Saturday night.

One father shared a story that was especially touching and impressive. It has to do with time together not having to be regimented and mechanical.

At age forty, this father had just about everything—professionally, that is. He was awarded a Ph.D. from Harvard at a very young age. He had become a full professor quickly by writing books, books, and more books very quickly.

But his life fell apart even more quickly. His wife packed her bags to leave him one Monday morning, and his best friend was buried on Tuesday. ("He died from writing nine books and drinking to steady his hand when he picked up the phone to dicker with his publishers or creditors.") His brother, who had developed throat cancer from the cigarettes he smoked to calm himself from overwork, had his larynx removed on Friday.

"I looked at their lives, and I cried. And then I looked at my life, and I cried." And he began to change.

First, he convinced his wife to come back home and give their marriage another try. Then, he scheduled free time for himself and time for his family. At first he wondered, "What will we do in this time?" And then he remembered, "The history of science, the history of human exploration, is full of examples of experiments or quests that began for no particular reason and ended up with marvelous results. Think about it! Christopher Columbus was simply looking for a way to connect Europe with the spice merchants in the Orient. But he accidentally stumbled onto something infinitely more valuable than pepper. He ran into America."

He decided that chatting with his young sons while they had snacks or holding the baby while his wife slept might be the beginning of a wonderful quest. And because he envisioned a new way to live, this story has a happy ending. His wife and he visited a family therapist and ironed out their difficulties, and the family got back on the right track.

People in strong families seem to sense that much of what they do to preserve and enrich their lives is done in their times together. So, do they spend a lot of time "doing nothing"? No. More precisely, they are not worried about being with each other with no particular goal in mind. They know that in the long run, good things happen as a result of shared times.

SERENDIPITY

Serendipity is a fun word. It means finding good things that were not sought. Much of the good that comes from time spent together is serendipitous. It springs naturally from the moment. It has been said that we as human beings should live each day "as if it were a prayer." Each moment of our lives together is a verse of this daily prayer. By living life from sacred moment to sacred moment, we are aware of the potential joy waiting to be found in each of these fleeting moments. Instead of being lost in the race to accomplish, we can find contentment now. Instead of striving to be fulfilled and happy after the race is run, we can enjoy the sunshine of our pleasant saunter through life.

Strong families enjoy being with each other. They invest a great deal of time into each other. And the most fun they have in life tends to come from these serendipitous moments.

I tried so hard to work and save money so we could have a long vacation in Europe. There I would be perfectly happy, I reasoned. But I drove myself to distraction. I never was where I wanted to be. I was always on the road to becoming. The goal was always far, far in the future. Finally, my wife looked at me one evening; I was slumped, exhausted in my living-room chair. "This is life, Warren," she said. "Not yesterday or tomorrow. Right now. Let's love each other right now, and tomorrow will fix itself." She was right. It did.

It was early spring at the beach and unexpectedly, bitterly cold. We decided to bundle up and take one short walk before going home. We drove a few miles to a section of Gulf Islands National Seashore, pulled into the empty parking lot, and were immediately greeted by a flock of seagulls. As we got out, we tossed some snack leftovers. In a flash, we were in a cloud of seagulls. Caught up in the fun of it, we fed the gulls a box of saltines, a loaf of bread, and a box of Moonpie cakes from our picnic supplies. They'd hover just above our heads and catch the goodies we tossed. I've never seen gulls so close; sometimes their wings brushed our hair.

SIX SUGGESTIONS ON HOW TO SPEND QUALITY TIME TOGETHER

Families benefit from shared time because it eases loneliness and isolation, nurtures relationships, and creates a family identity. And exactly what do strong families do when they're together? Just about anything and everything. Here are six suggestions as to how you can create quality family time in great quantities.

SUGGESTION #1—SHARE MEALS TOGETHER

Many, many times families mentioned that they eat meals together on a regular basis.

One Idaho mother told us:

We eat the evening meal together. In extreme cases, one of us may not be there, but everyone knows that being absent from dinner is not taken lightly. We use that time to share triumphs and tribulations. In a hectic world, we need some common ground where we can meet.

Another mother in North Carolina added:

We always eat dinner together and try to be together for breakfast as well. And we have a rule of no television during meals.

SUGGESTION #2—DO HOUSE AND YARD CHORES TOGETHER

One Louisiana man said:

I grew up on a farm, so maybe my background differs from some of the people you've talked with, but a lot of the time I shared with my parents was working time. I fed the animals, gathered eggs, weeded the garden, picked produce out of the garden, and generally helped around the house. It wasn't that I had a list of chores and worked alone. Dad and I would do the feeding; Mom and I would pick and prepare vegetables. We'd sweat and complain, laugh and talk as we worked.

Strong families have learned to turn the time necessary for running a household into opportunities to get together and communicate. Some of their comments illustrate this.

I work until late in the afternoon, so I need help getting dinner ready. At first my son protested about having to cook, but I've convinced him that there may be many times when knowing how to cook will be handy.

Now he's proud of his accomplishments. He often has cookies or a cake ready before I get home.

My daughter is still a little young to handle very hot things or knives, but she sets the table and likes to make simple vegetable or fruit salads.

We all get in the kitchen and talk about what went on at school and work while we fix dinner. They're learning other valuable things besides cooking; they're learning they are important in making our family run. That increases confidence and esteem.

When I find myself tempted to shoo the kids so I can get a job done faster without their "help," I remind myself that helping is how kids learn to do these things. My husband's father is a pretty decent mechanic, but my husband knows very little about cars. When he was young and eager to learn, his dad wouldn't let him help out. Dad wasn't being mean; he was just in a hurry to be done, didn't want J. D. to get dirty, wanted the job done just so, or didn't think a kid could really be interested.

SUGGESTION #3—PLAY TOGETHER

There are at least two places to have wonderful recreational times together: outside and inside. Let's think about both.

A large number of the strong families who participated in the research mentioned *outdoor* activities as favorite ways to be together. Many play catch or yard games. They camp, canoe, hike, picnic, stargaze, play league sports, bicycle, walk, and swim. Their responses give some clues to the allure of the outdoors.

We *love to canoe a little river not far from here. The appeal to me is the beauty of the spot. After a day of sunlight on the leaves, fresh air, the ripple of the water, my soul is refreshed. My husband says he feels more in touch with the eternally important things. He gains perspective. Petty trials come and go, but the river flows on. The kids have a blast swimming, collecting rocks, hunting fossils, and stalking frogs.*

We *have a special town on the Gulf Coast that is a favorite of ours. We camp and fish and go crabbing. There are no phones or televisions. For a couple of days, the outside world disappears. What a pleasure it is to get up when we want, eat when we're hungry, and be free of schedules.*

Many strong families also mentioned indoor recreation.

Every Friday night we rent some movies and make nachos.

We enjoy board games such as Monopoly or Scrabble, telling stories, or reading aloud as a change from television.

We do jigsaw puzzles as a family fun pursuit. The only problem is that it's hard to leave a good puzzle. Once or twice we've lost track of the time until 2:00 A.M., so we try to be really careful on school nights.

Some of the strong families spoke out against television; they feel that television interrupts and demands too much attention. As a result, some have strict limits on the amount of time spent watching, or they have banished the television to the basement to make it less accessible and have sought other leisure pursuits. Others have attempted to improve the time spent watching television. They turn down the volume during commercials and discuss what they've seen. Or they'll discuss the commercials with their children, asking questions such as "Do you think this product will make you happier, prettier, or more popular?"

SUGGESTION #4—ENJOY RELIGIOUS, CLUB, AND SCHOOL ACTIVITIES TOGETHER

For many strong families, weekly worship is a family event. What better way to spend time together than to spend it praising God. But when you do this, make an effort not to rise late, dress hurriedly, or fight on the way to church. Too many family memories of church revolve around stress and irritability. Instead, get up early. Breakfast leisurely. On the way to church talk about why you go, what you have to offer God, and what the worship should accomplish for each of you.

On the way home, discuss the kids' Bible classes. Ask them what the lesson was about, what they learned, and how they can apply what they learned to their everyday lives. Do the same with the sermon with those old enough to understand it.

Whatever you do, don't spend any time discussing church problems or dissecting church members. Make it a wonderful time of sharing God without any negatives to ruin the moment.

Make your religious family time broader than just Sunday. Make a special night during the week for home Bible instruction that includes a good dose of social skills and etiquette.

Barry Thompson, M.D., and his wife, Karen, of North Augusta, South Carolina, made a special night each week when their boys were growing up. First came a formal meal, for which the boys dressed up and used their best manners. When they finished the feast, they moved to the family room where Dad or Mom taught a Bible lesson of relevance to the family (or sometimes more of relevance to growing boys!).

They lit a special lamp and placed it in front of the speaker. When the lamp was placed in front of any person on those special nights, he or she could speak freely without interruption from anyone else in the room. When the formal presentation of the study was finished, the lamp would move around the room from person to person so each could give his views, understandings, and the like.

Not only did the boys learn the Word of God, they learned manners, respect, and proper etiquette at the same time!

In addition to activities involving spiritual growth, strong families report that activities at school, Scouting, and 4-H often involve the entire family as well. If the children have a band concert, recital, or are in a program, Mom and Dad and the family are in the audience.

One father told us, with great and obvious pride, of his adult daughter's recent recital. He had been attending an important conference but took a day out to fly across four states to attend her recital (and then flew back to the conference).

SUGGESTION #5—SPEND SPECIAL EVENTS TOGETHER

These include holidays, vacations, and personal observances such as birthdays. Members of strong families regard these as times when the entire family should be together.

Birthdays are big events at our home. We have a special meal and cake. The birthday person gets presents, of course. We also have added our own twist. The birthday person gives small presents to family members as a way of thanking them for enriching his or her life.

Holidays are special times. We enjoy decorating the house, fixing special foods. We have traditions for most holidays—jack-o'-lanterns at Halloween, a food basket to give to a needy family at Thanksgiving, sunrise service at Easter, a trip to the cemetery on Memorial Day.

Our vacations are planned with everyone in the family in mind. We try to work in antique or craft shops for Mom, some fishing for Dad, and amusement parks or swimming for the children.

SUGGESTION #6—DO NOTHING IN PARTICULAR

As you have read the previous suggestions for spending quality time together, you may have concluded that members of strong families are busy people—always *doing* something. Indeed, they do spend time doing many worthwhile things, but please remember this: We are human *beings*, not human *doings*.

Recognize the value and benefit of being with members of your family and not doing anything in particular. Sit on the deck in the late evening and watch fireflies; listen to the rain. Put some miles on a porch swing or rocking chairs. Meander along the creek or pond; wade a little; skip some stones. Stretch out in the grass and watch the clouds drift by or watch for shooting stars at night.

We don't have to do anything with each other to enjoy each other's company. We can be content doing nothing except savoring family closeness.

Here's how one family spent leisurely time together:

When I was growing up, there was a mimosa tree in our yard. It was large and umbrella-like, with fragrant pink flowers in the summer. We—Mom, Sis, and I—would spread a blanket under the tree, stretch out, and watch the hummingbirds that came for the nectar from its blossoms. You had to lie very still, and of course, you couldn't talk or the hummers wouldn't come. We spent many warm, drowsy afternoons lying there, doing nothing in particular.

THE ULTIMATE SHARING

The Sandhills are a vast area of grass-covered sand dunes in central and western Nebraska. For miles and miles, sand, wind, and sky dominate. The area is used for cattle grazing, but because it takes so much land to support one cow, the ranches are enormous. One woman from the Sandhills told about her thirty-seven-year marriage. She and her husband have spent their entire married life on several thousands of acres of short-grass prairie. Their nearest neighbor is ten miles away; the nearest community is fifty miles. To see a movie or buy groceries means a round trip of one hundred miles.

Their life is an ongoing mix of working on the ranch, rest, formal worship on Sunday, and an occasional visitor. Sometimes they go several days without seeing anyone but each other. One January blizzard buried them for three weeks before the snow plows dug them out.

Most people think we lead a hard and lonely life. This might be true if our situation were different. But we share so much—our love of this open, quiet country, our work making the ranch successful, and our special feelings for each other. We're more than married; we're best friends.

While the isolation of the Sandhills would sound foreign to many strong families, the essence of this Sandhills marriage would seem very familiar. Many of the husbands and wives in strong families indicate that they are intensely bound together; they share all (or nearly all) aspects of their lives with interest and joy. They are mates, lovers, companions, partners, and best friends. Some, like the Sandhills couple, share their work as well. The central satisfaction in their lives is their relationship. Many people might think this type of relationship is stifling or phony, but our strong families say this is not so. Their intimacy and sharing are genuine.

And this kind of sharing isn't just for husbands and wives.

"I don't have any idea what I did all day today," a New Mexico woman said with a smile, "but I was busy every second." Indeed, she no doubt was. This wife and mother has "temporarily retired" from teaching to rear her four children—all under age ten. Her day is a free-flowing whirlwind. Bright and busy children come up to her time and again for support, to show something they have made, to ask for help, or just because they are happy to be with her. Her philosophy is found in this anonymous poem framed on the hallway wall:

> Cleaning and scrubbing can wait 'til tomorrow,
> For babies grow up, we've learned to our sorrow—
> So quiet down, cobwebs, dust, go to sleep—
> I'm rocking my baby, and babies don't keep.

Babies don't keep. Neither do older children and marriages! Members of strong families have learned that it isn't enough to speak of commitment to the family or to plan to show it "someday." They must demonstrate that commitment now. Nowhere is their commitment more clearly demonstrated than in the amount of time they spend together.

THE BEST GIFT

Most of us spend time and money several times a year selecting perfect gifts for birthdays, anniversaries, or holidays for the people we love. The very best gift of all would take nothing from the bank account. And you wouldn't have to wrap it either.

If you believe, as do most people, that your life is the most valuable possession you have, then a piece of your life is the most precious gift you have to offer. We give that precious gift in the chunks of our time we give to our loved ones. The families in this research give generously of their lives to each other, and that is one important reason why they are so strong. They understand the great truth taught in Ephesians: "Be very careful, then, how you live—not as unwise but as wise, making the most of every opportunity, because the days are evil."[8]

Don't waste any more opportunities to spend quality time in great quantities with your family.

 ## Putting It to Work—Six Ideas for Your Family

1. *Take a journey of happy memories.* Close your eyes and think back to your childhood, wander through the memories, and bring back the three or four happiest. Could you create some similar experiences for your family?

2. *Set aside fifteen minutes when the kids come in from school to share a snack and talk.* If you can't be at home after school, save your break time at work to share their day over the phone.

3. *Designate one wall (or room) for family mementos.* Hang pictures of Mom and Dad, the kids, the pets, grandparents, houses you lived in before, favorite vacation spots, etc. Decorate the room with souvenirs of trips—shells from the beach, for example. The room may not win any awards for interior design, but the furnishings will have meaning for your family. A feeling of family identity will be created.

4. *Work together to design a family symbol or logo.* Have it printed on T-shirts or jackets so that everyone in the family has matching jackets or shirts. Put the design on a flag for the house or a banner for the front door.

5. *Write down or tape-record your family's history.* Involve grandparents and other older relatives. Ask grandparents questions such as "What were your parents' and grandparents' names?" "Where did they live?" "Where are they buried?" "Where did you live as a child?" "What occupations did these folks follow?" "Who are your brothers and sisters?" "How did you and your spouse meet, court, and marry?" "What are the names of your children? When and where were they born?" "Where did you attend school?" "How did you celebrate holidays, birthdays, harvests,

weddings, as a child?" For the immediate family include information about places of residence, circumstances surrounding the birth of each child, vacations, special events, and hobbies. Use pictures if possible. A family reunion can be a good place to find out interesting bits of family history.

6. *Plan opportunities for one-on-one relationships to grow.* For example, Nick occasionally takes Joseph to a movie; Nick and Nancy may attend a conference together while Joseph stays with his grandparents; David and Joseph play computer games together. It gives time for those separate relationships to be cultivated.

STEP FIVE
NURTURE SPIRITUAL WELL-BEING

Ted and Nell's life together seemed storybook perfect. They'd been happily married for twelve years, they had two lovely daughters, he was advancing in his profession, the family was close and loving, and they enjoyed their life in a pleasant southern city. Then Nell began having a persistent backache. Several trips to the doctor and extensive testing led to surgery, and that revealed renal cell carcinoma—a vicious cancer that spreads like wildfire.

Ted and Nell made repeated trips to Houston for cobalt treatments and chemotherapy. They prayed. Nell's gravest concern was that she wouldn't get to rear her girls. Ted and Nell grew closer together, uniting to meet the challenge of her illness. But her physical condition continued to deteriorate. Six months after her surgery, she quietly passed from this life in her sleep at home.

Ted talked about their experience and belief: "I hoped and prayed for something good to come out of this. I believe in God. I believe he is in control. I believe it is in his power to intervene in human disaster. Why he didn't intervene for us, I don't know. Life and death are such integral parts of the human condition that we can hardly feel we were unfairly chosen for tragedy. In our twelve years of marriage, we had many good things.

"Everything that Nell and I shared—our lives together, our closeness, how we learned to face the challenge of her illness, even her death—all of that is part of me now. And I try to share what's important about it with other people."

Ted feels most compelled to share one particular incident because of its profound effect on him. As Nell neared the time of her passing, Ted was sitting beside her on the bed with tears streaming down his face. Nell opened her eyes and said something that made a lasting impact on Ted.

"Don't worry about me. I will be all right," she said. "Whatever happens; I will be with God, and I will be all right."

She seemed to sense the question spinning in Ted's mind. "We don't know why this has happened," she comforted, "but we do know that God has a plan for our family. We've always believed that. When I go, you will still have the children. They will need you, and you will need them. God's great purpose will still be working through you and the children."

Nell's words gave Ted courage, comfort, and a new perspective. "I felt more at peace about everything," Ted said. "What she said helped me remember that I had something important to live for because we were each an important part of God's plan for our family."

Beyond Ted's faith in God's plan for his life on earth, he also knew that this life was not the end. "Our belief in God and our belief that life is eternal was a great comfort and help to both Nell and me throughout this experience. I know I'll see her again."[1]

SPIRITUAL WELL-BEING MAKES A FAMILY STRONG

Ted and Nell's faith in God, and how that faith carried their family through a difficult time, exemplifies the blessings of building a family on a spiritual foundation.

Even though not all the strong families in the the Family-Strengths Research Project share the Christian faith, it's amazing that the need for spirituality and a belief in a "higher power" was evident to them all. Families all over the world, from a variety of cultures, recognized the reality of a power outside themselves.

SIX BLESSINGS OF BUILDING YOUR "HOUSE" ON A SPIRITUAL FOUNDATION

The importance of a spiritual center can't be overstated when it comes to strong families. Reliance upon a power above and beyond themselves was the glue that held these families together and made them strong. Jesus, in the book of Matthew, talks about the importance of building our "house" on the right foundation. "Therefore everyone who hears these words of mine and puts them into practice is like a wise man who built his house on the rock. The rain came down, the streams rose, and the winds blew and beat against that house; yet it did not fall, because it had its foundation on the rock."[2] Ted and Nell felt the impact of the rains and the storm and the winds that beat against their family. Yet because their house was built on a firm, spiritual foundation, it weathered the storm and stood firm.

The blessings of building your house on a spiritual foundation are endless. Following are six of the many.

BLESSING #1—PURPOSE OR MEANING

"What is life all about?"

"Why am I here?"

Members of strong families ask themselves these questions—just as the rest of humanity does. The feeling that our lives are serving a purpose contributes immeasurably to overall satisfaction. A businessman from Texas told us of his search for meaning:

I started my adult life with a bang, you might say. My parents were moderately well-to-do and gave me a good start in my own business. It flourished, and things looked rosy for ten years or so. Then the economy went sour at about the time I had made some risky investments. One by one, those went down the tubes. In the end we lost everything—house, cars, and the business.

My wife and I sat out by the lake one night and talked until the sun came up. I remember feeling stripped of everything—as if I'd been robbed. "Why try again?" I asked her. "We may work and work only to lose it." We struggled with that a long time and finally decided that we had been thinking wrong. We'd been so occupied with making money and the daily "busy-ness" of life that we'd allowed God and people to be crowded out of our lives.

We reminded ourselves that the purpose of life isn't to accumulate money, swimming pools, cars, and fur coats. The purpose of life is to love and honor God and to express God's love toward each other. We decided to take time to grow closer to God, to enjoy life—because it is such a precious gift. We began to make it a priority to cherish our family and friends and to help other people.

The investments of time and effort we make in family and friends, in church, in charitable work, and in improving ourselves can never be lost. Things in the mind and heart can't be taken away.

We did start over again and have enjoyed success. We've replaced many of the material things we lost, but most importantly, we have changed our thoughts. The job, the possessions, the money are no longer an end in themselves. They are a means of making life pleasant and serving God and others. If I lost them all tomorrow I'd still feel rich.

BLESSING #2—GUIDELINES FOR LIVING

When we asked how spiritual well-being contributes to family strength, quite a few families told us that the most important way was by providing guidelines for living.

The principles that Jesus taught and the values found throughout the Bible are helpful in creating good family relationships. By that I mean that things such as responsibility, concern for others, empathy, love, forgiveness, honesty, controlling anger, gentleness, and patience are all taught as virtues. What a wonderful map for successful and loving relationships!

It is so simple, yet so powerful! One of the best and most concise guides for having good relationships is found in the book of Matthew. Jesus tells us to treat others as we would like them to treat us.[3] We really try to apply this rule in our family. It has been a great help to us as we have taught our children how to get along with others (including brothers and sisters!).

Our family is so blessed by the marvelous and wonderful love of God. We remind ourselves often that God loves us even though we are not perfect and even though we often act unloveable and make dumb mistakes. Just thinking about that kind of love and how wonderful God is helps me be more patient and kind. It helps me love my husband and son even when I don't like what they're doing.

The belief that we are not alone helps us deal with conflict and anger. We believe we have divine guidance to show us the best way when we disagree.

These strong families believe that God has established moral absolutes and that he is interested in what we do from day to day. When people believe in these basic truths and abide by them, their lives have direction and they can know what is right and what is wrong. They have learned the value of putting into practice the principles taught in the Bible. As James said, "Do not merely listen to the word, and so deceive yourselves. Do what it says."[4]

Families with strong spiritual well-being know that God is there, watching, caring, loving, and guiding. And they know that they can turn to God at any time for guidance, as James 1:5 says, "If any of you lacks wisdom, he should ask God, who gives generously to all without finding fault, and it will be given to him."

BLESSING #3—FREEDOM AND PEACE

Lowell is a pharmacist who was storming through life, full speed ahead, until a heart attack followed by triple bypass surgery felled him.

He told about his discovery of freedom:

Lying there on that hospital bed, I realized something important and said to myself, "Well, it's in God's hands now." And I knew it wasn't just the operation and the doctors and all that—it was me. I was in God's hands, and I'll tell you, for a man like me (or like I was then), that's a tough thing to admit. Because, you see, I had always thought God wanted me to be in charge; and boy, was I in charge! I was the most in charge fellow you ever saw back in those days. And when I had that heart attack, it threw me. I couldn't figure out why God let that happen to me when I was trying my best to manage everything he'd given me. I was a pretty good manager, too, if I do say so.

I'd always felt that everything I had—my family and my friends—were direct gifts from God. But to wind up flat on my back with the doctor telling me I had to slow down and think about letting some other people take care of some of my responsibilities—well, it was a hard thing for me.

I've always been a Christian—ever since I was a kid. My folks were practicing Christians—they lived at home the way most people only live on Sundays—and I've tried to raise my family that way too. But I've probably never doubted the presence of Christ in my life as much as I did right after the heart attack. It just didn't make sense to me! I thought I knew what I was doing and that I was doing what God had in mind for me.

During the week after my heart attack and before the bypass surgery, I was almost crazy with anger and fear. I had so many plans, and this cheated me out of them. I was afraid I would die. I'd lie in bed listening to the beep of the heart monitor, wondering how it would be to hear it quit.

Faith, to me, is what happens when you can't make sense of life yourself. Then you have to wait, and God gives you the understanding. At least, he did for me. I guess it took me the better part of a week to realize that what he wanted was for me to hand him the keys and let him be boss again.

As soon as I surrendered control, I felt a flood of relief—from fear, from anger, from anxiety. I knew with complete confidence that God *would care for me—whether I lived or died, whether I went back to work or not. The peace of that realization is enormous.*

Lowell made excellent physical and emotional recovery. He feels better than he has in many years and works a reasonable schedule once again. By turning to God, Lowell found freedom from fear, anger, and anxiety. He found peace.

Peace even in the face of trial. That's hard to explain to those who don't have a spiritual relationship with God, but it gets strong affirmation from those who do. "The peace of God, which transcends all understanding, will guard your hearts and your minds in Christ Jesus."[5]

A Kansas woman told us of her revelation about peace:

I was having one of those particularly difficult times. Everything seemed to be going wrong at work; my folks weren't doing well health-wise. A routine physical had turned up a lump in my breast. Naturally, all I could imagine was cancer.

Partly to distract myself, I went to a shopping center and was meandering through a gift shop when I saw a plaque that said:

Sometimes God stills the storm
To calm his frightened child.
Sometimes he lets the storm rage
And calms his child instead.

I immediately bought it and went home. Two possibilities awaited me—either my troubles would clear up or God would strengthen and quiet me to meet them. Either way I didn't have to worry or be afraid.

Of course, that's what God wants us to have, freedom from anxiety because of our relationship with him. Through Paul he said, "Do not be anxious about anything, but in everything, by prayer and petition, with thanksgiving, present your requests to God."[6] Through Peter he said, "Cast all your anxiety on him because he cares for you."[7]

Freedom from worry, anger, anxiety, and fear is not the only freedom that spiritual well-being brings to strong families. Many report a freeing from guilt and low self-esteem.

I believe that I will be forgiven if I can forgive others.[8] *It's similar to the law of physics about every action having an equal reaction. If I forgive I am forgiven. So I don't have to carry around a load of guilt.*

The intrinsic value of each person is such a strong part of my religious belief. I know people make mistakes, but they are valuable anyway. We don't earn God's love, but we must be worthwhile or he wouldn't love us.

I like the analogy of a human body in thinking about the importance of each person.[9] *Each of us has talents and skills. My talent may be less than yours or greater than someone else's. It doesn't matter. We each have a contribution to make. The whole body can't be "eyes"—some parts have to be "ears" or "feet"—and it takes all the parts working together to make the body complete.*

Believing that God loves us, no matter what, and that he has gifted different people in different ways gives members of strong families a peace with self. "I am lovable, just the way God made me!"

BLESSING #4—A POSITIVE, CONFIDENT OUTLOOK

A belief that life has meaning and purpose helps members of strong families to maintain their perspective. They aren't completely overwhelmed by temporary troubles. Their outlook on life stays positive and confident. One New England mother said,

Our religious beliefs give us a great sense of confidence. We know we are not alone and do not have to depend upon ourselves completely. God is in our lives.

Joan's ten-year-old son was killed in an accident at a church ice-cream social. She talked at length about the people and factors that helped her through that terrible time. She concluded,

One song went over and over in my head; the meaning of the hymn is that God is with me and will help me cope, give me strength. I never, ever felt that I couldn't get through. Many people came up to me and said, "We lost a child too." And I'd think, Hey, they made it. So can I.

Bob and Vernita Garriott decided early in their marriage to face life with a positve, confident outlook. After meeting at a small college in Oklahoma, they courted and decided to marry. But unlike most couples, they decided (after long and prayerful consideration) *not* to have biological children. Why? Vernita is legally blind due to a hereditary trait. Bob was born with only a left arm. They didn't want to pass along any genetic liabilities. They decided to adopt children instead.

So they finished undergraduate degrees in education and sociology. And when they felt they were ready for parenthood, they applied to adopt a child. Almost immediately, they ran into barriers. "How will you be able to feed a baby?" they asked Vernita. "What if you get your hands dirty changing a messy diaper?" Vernita responded that she thought hand washing a good idea after diapering—even for people with excellent vision.

But their efforts to adopt were stalled, delayed, or diverted for almost two years. Civil rights legislation was enacted, and eventually they were offered a child with special needs. A charming little guy— Kristian—needed a home. He had been born without feet or fingers; the development of his limbs had stopped at that point. He also had a cleft palate, was missing 80 percent of his tongue, and had cranial nerve damage, causing his face to be partially paralyzed.

Bob and Vernita spent much time in prayer, considering whether they should adopt Kristian. They had felt guided by God to adopt children. Perhaps he wanted them to parent children with special needs. After all, their personal experience and professional training (by this time, Bob had completed his master's degree in vocational rehabilitation) made them uniquely qualified. And their generous, loving hearts made them willing. Years later, Vernita would laugh, "They didn't think I could see well enough to feed a normal baby, so they gave me one who required special bottles and nipples because of his cleft palate! Figure that one out!"

Kristian grew and flourished—even with numerous surgeries. He was an active preschooler when Ricky joined the family. Ricky had several strokes during his birth, resulting in permanent brain damage.

Ricky also added another dimension to their family. He is of African-American descent. "We were criticized by folks at church and within our family," Vernita explains. "They didn't think we should cross racial lines. And they argued that we wouldn't be able to help Ricky much because he was retarded."

But the Garriotts were guided by a belief that God's plan for them was to help people who were at risk or who were difficult to love. They adopted Kevin, a troubled teen who had come to them in foster care. Eventually, the Garriotts came in contact with Holt International Children's Services, a Christian agency devoted to helping homeless children around the world. Through Holt, they learned about a young man in the Philippines who needed a home, and so sixteen-year-old Domingo came into the family. Not long after that, they adopted Becky, a young girl who had been in foster care most of her fourteen years. Her birth mother was suspected of having thrown her from a moving car when she was eighteen months old. As a result of her injuries, Becky has some mild cognitive difficulties and is prone to seizures. "But Becky has the distinction of being our only daughter," observes Vernita. When Becky made some mistakes in judgment and became pregnant, Bob and Vernita adopted her baby, Nikki Joe.

Not long after that, Holt International asked Bob and Vernita if they would consider taking other children. Bob and Vernita were approaching the age limit for adoptive parents, but Holt ministries sought them out because they were the best couple for the job. And so Victor, a tiny, blind baby from Guatemala; Kyle, a street orphan from Brazil; and Mark, a severely burned child from Thailand, joined their family. "Things had come full circle," Vernita said. "In the beginning, we were told we weren't capable of caring for children, and now we were being sought out."

Over a twenty-year period, the Garriotts have opened their hearts and home to hundreds of foster children and disabled adults.

How have they managed? They have a deep and abiding conviction that the work they are doing is of great value. "We haven't done this alone. God is always with us, and we've had help from many Christian friends."

Bob and Vernita are people of faith. They are active in their church, and the children are involved in church activities. Bible study and prayer are a daily part of their lives. Their steadfast faith has guided them in their choices and spurred them on when things got tough. Bob and Vernita show the rest of us what it means to build a house on a spiritual foundation.

BLESSING #5—SUPPORT FROM LIKE-MINDED PEOPLE

One of the benefits of building your house on a spiritual foundation is being part of a church family. In addition to the support found in our physical families, the fellowship and support from people in our extended spiritual family is invaluable. Ike and Meg in New Mexico get a great deal of pleasure out of their biweekly Bible-study group. Several couples gather for a potluck meal (at a different home on a rotating basis) and then share in a free-flowing discussion. "Last time we talked about what it means to turn the other cheek," Meg explained.

Besides a lively discussion on an important moral or ethical question, the couples gain the pleasure of a night of "adult" company. (A teenager is paid to keep the younger children at a nearby location or in another room.) They are in the company of other people committed to family and to things of the spirit. The food is good, the laughter is genuine, and it doesn't cost much. They gain spiritual and emotional strength from each other.

A mother from Kentucky told us of the help she received from people at church:

This happened a long time ago—fifteen years, I guess, by now. Our family has come a long way since then because of a wonderful group of people. They don't think of themselves as extraordinary, and they'd tell you they were only doing what was right. Here's what they did for us.

My husband and I married too young and had Jenny too soon. (Hindsight is always clear, you know.) I found myself in a tiny, dingy trailer with a demanding infant. Bill's job kept him away long hours. I didn't have any friends in the community. Alone and overwhelmed, I slipped into clinical depression. I'd be so depressed I couldn't move; it would take all my effort to change Jen's diaper and stick a bottle of formula in her mouth. I couldn't cook or clean. Bill would bathe Jen, wash diapers, and tidy up when he came home, but he couldn't keep up with it. Finally, he asked some ladies at the congregation for help.

Three of the more mature women—grandmothers, all of them—took turns coming to the trailer. They cleaned and cooked, did laundry, and took care of Jenny. She needed the rocking and cuddling; they helped me to see that I had to get well to rear her. And I learned a lot of practical stuff by watching how they managed time and paced themselves.

As soon as I began to feel a tiny bit better, we were invited by another young couple to their home for dinner and cards. I didn't want to go, but everyone insisted. I felt better after. The next week another family had us over for dinner. Soon I had some friends.

Someone telephoned every day to see how we were. Ladies stopped by for coffee and conversation or to go shopping. As I improved, the intensive care—the ladies who came over every day—slacked off to let me resume what I could. Eventually, they didn't have to come. But the friendships stayed. We are still close to two couples we grew to know during that time. Time and distance separate us now—one couple lives in Dallas, the other in Boston—but we write and telephone and occasionally vacation with each other. We truly are brothers and sisters in spirit.

Other strong family members told us of support and aid from people of their church families during illnesses, births of babies, deaths, and natural disasters such as fires or floods. And even during good times, the contact with like-minded people is a source of encouragement, a reminder of values, and a model for conduct.

Sounds almost like the church in the New Testament, doesn't it? (See Acts 2:44–47.)

BLESSING #6—ACCESS TO THE POWER OF GOD

The power available to families with true spiritual well-being isn't limited just to what they *feel* or *believe* when they face the occasional tribulations of the trials of life. While their faith and confidence give strength and hope, they know that the power does not lie within themselves. They know that the power of God transcends all that is human. There really is one who holds supernatural understanding, supernatural love, and supernatural power to reach into our lives and do for us those things that only he can do.

And the faith of strong families isn't just faith in a religious system; it is in the Lord of lords and King of kings. Those whose spiritual well-being comes from a relationship with God know that "The Lord Almighty is with us."[10]

They believe, not only that God exists, but that he will do what he says he will do: "Without faith it is impossible to please God, because anyone who comes to him must believe that he exists and that he rewards those who earnestly seek him."[11]

Strong Christian families recognize God's involvement in their lives and praise him for it.

> Praise be to the name of God for ever and ever; wisdom and power are his. He changes times and seasons; he sets up kings and deposes them. He gives wisdom to the wise and knowledge to the discerning. He reveals deep and hidden things; he knows what lies in darkness, and light dwells with him. I thank and praise you, O God of my fathers: You have given me wisdom and power, you have made known to me what we asked of you.[12]

> Praise him for his acts of power; praise him for his surpassing greatness.[13]

FROM THEORY TO PRACTICE

The strong families interviewed for this research shared more than just the "theory" behind their faith; they also shared the "nuts and bolts" of how their family members expressed their spiritual dimension and how they nurtured spiritual well-being in their family. What they shared fell into six broad categories.

1. TRADITIONS AND RITUALS

One of the most apparent demonstrations of the spiritual nature is participation in religious traditions and rituals. Tradition and ritual have been criticized at times as being mechanical and meaningless—empty motion. Certainly that can be the case. But for strong families, tradition and ritual are outward expressions of a deeper commitment. The following remarks were typical:

We attend worship services each week as a family. We sit together.

We started a tradition in our family when our children reached junior high and we realized how bad the alcohol and other drug problems were getting in school and how much peer pressure they face each day. We have family devotionals at breakfast each morning. We felt these established a tone and reminded the children each morning of what we believed.

My husband and I have always been active in our local congregation. It's important to us as a source of renewal and as one way we teach our children.

Of course we attend worship services each week, but the holidays are a special time to reaffirm our beliefs, because many holidays are basically religious in origin. Christmas, Easter, Thanksgiving—all have spiritual meaning in our home. Furthermore, the major milestones in our family are marked by religious observances. We were married by a minister in a chapel. Each of our children was blessed and dedicated as an infant; later they were confirmed in the church. We hope they will be married in a religious ceremony. Deaths are noted by funerals conducted by the church.

2. RELIGIOUS HERITAGE

Religious or spiritual history and heritage provide guidelines for living, good models for character development, and a sense of belonging to a larger group. Strong families also indicate an awareness of their spiritual heritage in the celebration of holidays.

We have a rich spiritual heritage that we rely on for support and guidance. We believe and read the Bible, and we read other Christian literature, as well. Stories of spiritual leaders and missionaries and inspirational stories, for example, have timeless truths for living the best way. We've tried to use those to guide our lives.

A couple of years ago we celebrated the Passover meal. We are Christians, but we wanted to tap into some of our religious history. We roasted lamb, made a salad of greens and herbs, and fixed unleavened bread. We told the story of the Israelites in Egyptian slavery, of Moses and the plagues. So many of our symbols—Christ as the sacrificial lamb, deliverance from the bondage of sin, and the unleavened bread of communion—come from then. I feel that an unseen chain binds us back through time and space to those people and events and their beliefs.

Our children enjoy stories about heroes. We've tried to make sure that the heroes they learn about have traits that make them good models. As a result we rely heavily on Bible characters.

3. PRAYER AND MEDITATION

A man in Pennsylvania relates the story of how he and his wife started a family business:

We opened our business with little more than a dream and a great deal of faith. We borrowed most of the money to start; the building wasn't much to look at. Some of our friends and relatives didn't think we had a chance of making it. But we hung in there. At first it was just my wife and me working very long hours. Then in a few years, we were able to hire part-time help. After a few more years, we moved into a new, larger establishment. Sure, there were hard and discouraging times. There were moments when we thought that if we had good sense we would have quit long ago.

But we didn't quit, and the business became very successful.

I believe the most important reasons for what you do and the way you feel come from God. So we put together a simple formula for dealing with problems and overcoming our difficulties, both in our business and in our individual, personal lives. We practice this on a day-to-day basis, and it really has worked wonders for us. We highly recommend it.

In two, simple words, the formula is pray *and* visualize. *Prayer is the most effective way of making the connection between myself and the great source of all life and power—God. For us, prayer is a daily practice of talks and meditation with God. We talk to God as a loving friend, not as a distant, unconcerned presence. Most of the prayers are short, and we use everyday language—not* thee *and* thou.

I start the day with a prayer of praise in the early morning as I jog. We pray as we drive to and from work. We ask God to show us how to deal with specific situations. We say, for example, "God, give us your fresh insight in this matter of..." We often pray as a family.

After I have prayed, I visualize in my mind a good, positive outcome for everyone. I then put it completely in God's hands, and I don't worry about it.

You know, your life just goes better when you get in touch with the unlimited resources of God's great wisdom, love, and peace.

A Texas couple told us,

We join in family prayer each evening. We pray for each other, for guidance for our decisions, and for help with our problems. This puts us on a higher level of thinking and opens new dimensions for us. Our family becomes a circle of power; prayer energizes us.

A man from the Colorado mountains said,

I like to spend some time every day or so in meditation and prayer. Sometimes, I take a walk in the woods and marvel at the wonder of growing things or the steady progression of the seasons. Golden autumn leaves, the way mushrooms pop up overnight, and the songs of birds are all miracles of a sort. My thoughts are of praise to God for his wonderful creation. What an artist he is!

It is not surprising that strong families report that prayer and meditaion are valuable ways to access the power of God and to increase their spirituality. Consider what humankind was told a long time ago.

> Do not let this Book of the Law depart from your mouth; meditate on it day and night, so that you may be careful to do everything written in it. Then you will be prosperous and successful.[14]

> Within your temple, O God, we meditate on your unfailing love.[15]

> Oh, how I love your law! I meditate on it all day long. Your commands make me wiser than my enemies, for they are ever with me. I have more insight than all my teachers, for I meditate on your statutes.[16]

> Therefore let everyone who is godly pray to you while you may be found.[17]

> Watch and pray so that you will not fall into temptation. The spirit is willing, but the body is weak.[18]

> Pray continually; give thanks in all circumstances, for this is God's will for you in Christ Jesus.[19]

> Do not be anxious about anything, but in everything, by prayer and petition, with thanksgiving, present your requests to God.[20]

4. EVERYDAY LIFE

All the talk of religious belief, spiritual heritage, and faith would be only empty talk were it not for the fact that strong families primarily express their spirituality in everyday life. They literally practice what they preach.

Dr. Gay Vela invested countless hours examining the connection between family strengths and spirituality.[21] Gay wanted to look at families representing a wide variety of religious perspectives, and she was quite successful in this endeavor.

She talked with each family as a whole, and she talked with each of the individuals in the families separately. In these families, spirituality was alive and well and pervaded day-to-day life in the following ways:

◆ Commitment to the family and commitment to the sacred were closely related.

◆ Appreciation and affection were readily expressed in families where there was a faith in the Divine.

◆ Positive communication ruled where God was defined as the source of goodness and kindness.

◆ Time together came easier, for spiritual values were more important than material values.

◆ The ability to cope with stress and crisis flowed from a sense that life has meaning and purpose and that things, somehow, work out as they are meant to be.

Members of strong Christian families report an awareness of God's presence in their everyday lives.

I talk to God as I would to a friend, for I feel he is always near.

We believe that God is always present, guiding our lives in ways that are best for us.

Spiritual well-being is a very personal, practical, day-to-day matter in strong families. Religion is neither superficial ritual nor highly theoretical theology. Again, statements from strong families give insight into the meaning of this.

We are committed to a spiritual lifestyle that is livable. Maybe that's because we're practical people by nature. The beauty is that so many Christian teachings are very practical if you only give them a chance. Take, for example, the teaching that when we are angry we are not to sin.[22] *We aren't told not to get angry; that's very unrealistic. We are told to manage the anger, and that's excellent advice. Temper tantrums, unresolved resentment, and uncontrolled conflict can be very damaging to the individual and to relationships.*

Our family has certain values: honesty, responsibility, and tolerance, to name a few. But we have to practice those in everyday life. I can't talk about honesty and cheat on my income tax return. I can't yell responsibility and turn my back on a neighbor who needs help. I'd know I was a hypocrite, and so would the kids and everyone else.

The most recent conversation in our house has been about our television-watching habits. We—as a family—are evaluating how much we watch and what we watch. If a half-minute commercial can convince us to buy a certain toothpaste or cereal, doesn't it seem logical that a whole show can convince us to buy certain habits? We don't condone excessive drinking, marital infidelity, sex outside of marriage, smoking, or violence. What influence does it have on our lives to watch all that on TV? I don't mean to get on a soapbox here, but this is a good example of how we try to apply our spiritual values to real life.

5. STUDY

An ongoing study of God's Word is another way that members of strong Christian families nurture spiritual well-being. They rely primarily on the Bible, but also use the writings and commentary of others. Bible study may be done in classes at church, in informal neighborhood groups, in the home as a family, as individuals, or in a number of other ways.

I really look forward to my Sunday morning class at church. We have several teachers, and they are all excellent—always well prepared. We have looked at several topics that have really interested me, such as the role of women in the church. Our discussions are lively, and I'm learning so much.

My husband spends time reading the Bible every evening. He often asks our boys to sit and listen as he reads aloud. He may comment on what he has read or ask them what they think. It doesn't take long, but they are learning some every day.

Several summers ago, our family attended a Bible camp in the Black Hills area. The camp was out in a beautiful, remote area. There was a little stream that the kids waded and played in; we caught a grass snake. We had Bible classes and a program (lecture, music, devotional) each evening. The teens usually had a campfire with inspirational stories and singing late in the evening. I'll never forget how thrilling it was to be outside with the stars so bright and clear and to hear the teens singing "Our God, He Is Alive."

6. AVOIDING DISSENSION

When good communication is presented as a characteristic of strong families, someone always asks, "Do they ever fight?" It is natural to expect that a similar question might be asked about spirituality: Do they ever disagree?

Yes (to both questions).

Yes, but in ways that are constructive and creative.

Members of strong families recognize that squabbling over theological details or matters of opinion brings heartache and animosity—not the hope, joy, and comfort that spirituality should bring. Disagreement that grows to dissension destroys the atmosphere of spiritual well-being in a family. And yet, even folks in strong Christian families may disagree. So, what do they do then?

Many have realized the need to reduce or defuse destructive dissension. One way to reduce disagreement is to seek to understand each other's point of view. Be open to the idea of studying about the issue. Ask questions, and then listen to the answers.

Other strong family members spoke of the need to focus on shared beliefs.

My wife and I grew up in churches that seemed quite different from each other. We soon discovered that our conversations were more pleasant when we focused on areas of agreement. And do you know what? We agree on more than we don't. And, more important, we agree on the major issues.

Our family is relatively new to this community, and a neighbor invited us to worship services at her church. It is a large congregation and offers many activities that our teens immediately wanted to join. They came out of morning worship asking if we could come back that evening. This congregation is a bit different from what we have been accustomed to, so my first reaction was to think, No, we won't attend here. But the teens really wanted to go, so we visited several more times. It is true that they do two or three things differently than I would prefer, but the basic beliefs are exactly the same as mine. And the kids are always ready to go to services on time, and they're studying their Bibles at home. I've never seen them so enthusiastic and involved.

Respect for the person who disagrees is crucial to reducing dissension. In areas where family members cannot agree, strong families often decide to "agree to disagree." Both recognize and acknowledge that they just see things differently. They do not get caught up in judging each other, criticizing, or character assassination.

Many ministers and counselors have heard terrible stories of how bickering over spiritual questions has become a nightmare in a family or church. Because spiritual well-being is so crucial to family strength, each person should be encouraged to search out and find the faith that brings him or her personally to the throne of God. Establish the prime relationship with God first. Then, seek to understand others and to treat them with respect. Finally, be ready to forgive others and yourself for being human.

An Episcopal priest said it much better than we ever could. In a marriage-enrichment seminar, the priest was discussing the importance of spiritual values for family mental health. "I don't go to church anymore," one young husband said, challenging the priest. "Church is full of hypocrites."

The priest was too old and too wise to get in a fight. In fact, he understood exactly what the young man was saying, and in many ways could empathize with him. The priest smiled: "There's always room for one more hypocrite in church," he whispered.

The group of couples got very quiet for a few seconds and then they all roared with laughter. The young man and the priest laughed as heartily as anyone in the room. The priest had pointed out the obvious. He knew that the young man was searching for something sacred, and that his searching was a good sign. The young man was going in the right direction.

For that precious moment, the whole group was united in laughter and united in their natural goodness as human beings, their natural pettiness and jealousies, their natural hypocrisies, and their innate capacity to become one with God.

ALL YOU NEED

Earlier in this chapter you read some of thoughts from Joan, whose ten-year-old son was killed in an accident at an ice-cream social. Joan's husband, Bruce, is a minister, and the death of their son was a severe trial and torment to him. He reread all his old funeral sermons, searching for solace over Andy's death. Finding no satisfactory answers, he returned to Chicago, where he had attended seminary years before. He spent long hours with his mentors, the men who had helped him become a minister. "There is no answer to the question of why Andy died," they told him. "God is with you. That is all you need. The real agony—the real wilderness—is not pain or suffering or disappointment or even death.

"The real agony is the absence of God."

Members of strong Christian families would agree: The challenges and trials of life are bearable and surmountable because of the spiritual resources they tap. Without a relationship with God to give lasting meaning, life would lack purpose and direction; and these families would suffer alienation and despair. Instead, they feel a connection with God, and that gives them perspective, hope, optimism, and confidence.

Sustained by their faith in God, members of strong families find themselves encouraged by acts of kindness and the support of others. Freed from the burden of low self-esteem, they can see themselves and their possibilities clearly. With guilt and anxiety removed, they can be loving, open, accepting, and forgiving with others. Worship renews them, prayers comforts and energizes them, and God is with them. That is all they need.

Putting It to Work—Six Ideas for Your Family

1. *Set aside fifteen to thirty minutes each day for meditation and prayer.* Take a walk to get away from phones and interruptions; worship in the beauty of nature. Pray as you drive to work. Listen to an audio tape of the Bible as you drive or do chores. Meditate on the Word of God.

2. *Join a discussion group* (or form one with your friends) to consider religious topics, value-related matters, or philosophical issues.

3. *Use the Bible and its wonderful life lessons to help your children clarify their values.* Together discuss what is most important in life: work, health, money, popularity? Help them gain perspective. For example, you can teach them the world isn't over because they don't have a date this weekend.

4. *Identify weaknesses and strengths.* Begin with three of your personal weaknesses (lack of patience, poor temper control, worrying too much, for example). Decide how to improve in these areas, and then put your plan to work. Select three of your strengths (neighborliness, compassion, honesty, etc.), and make a conscious effort to develop these traits more fully.

   Now apply this exercise to the family unit. What are three areas of spiritual well-being where the family needs to devote some attention (attend church services more regularly, have more patience with each other, etc.)? Then discuss three areas of spiritual strength in the family (hospitality, daily family prayer, etc.).

5. *Have family devotionals on a regular basis.* Read Bible stories or other inspirational material, pray, sing, count your blessings, reaffirm your love and commitment to each other. Keep devotionals

short and varied so that the interest of children is stimulated rather than squelched.

6. *Volunteer your time and muscle and money to a cause.* You can do this as individuals and as a family unit. Most churches have benevolence programs that need volunteers to do things like pack food boxes or sort clothes for distribution to needy families. Consider being a foster parent. Help at Special Olympics. Organize or help at a free or low-cost medical clinic. Join in the collection of relief supplies for the victims of natural disasters. Find where Habitat for Humanity is building a house in your community.

STEP SIX

LEARN TO COPE
WITH STRESS AND CRISES

I can't think of anything more humiliating than to be thrown out of college in my sophomore year for cursing one of our seniors. In the small Christian college I attended, cursing was an enormous offense. What made it worse was that I did it in a crowd of students. What made it even worse than that was that I was a Bible major. What made it catastrophic was that one of my Bible professors was standing behind me as I threw my profane fit.

"Maybe I should have gotten a clue from the rapid disappearance of the anger on the face of the guy I was verbally abusing. He quit scowling and actually started to grin. At first I thought it was because he was twice my size and he'd just decided to beat me senseless. That just made me madder, so I pulled out a few choice words I'd been saving up since learning them in a summer warehouse job.

"That's when I felt the tap on my shoulder.

"I whirled, ready to enlarge the battle, and found myself staring directly into the eyes of Dr. Lawrence Barclay, our biblical languages professor. Drolly, he deadpanned, 'Having a bad day?'

"I didn't make a sound. Not even a muted, desperate groan, which I think all present would have excused. I just stood there with my mouth hanging open. The scenario of my impending doom flashed through my mind: the call to my parents, their six-hour trek to collect me, and the six-hour death march home. My life was over, and there wasn't a thing I could do about it.

"Dr. Barclay crooked his finger, mumbling something about following him, and headed off to his office. I remember the total silence in the hall of the rotunda as I passed the gaggle of students who'd witnessed the whole thing. They apparently were still in shock to hear a Bible major speak in what on our campus was an 'unknown tongue.' That, coupled with the awe of seeing a perpetrator caught in the act, prevented any talk or whispering—and very little breathing.

"Dr. Barclay slid easily into his chair and motioned for me to take the one opposite his desk. Once I was settled and finally had the courage to look up, I saw he was watching me. I was surprised by what I saw in his eyes. He wasn't angry, indignant, or coldly clinical. Instead, his eyes showed compassion. After a few moments, he asked me what had been going on in my life the last several days.

"I didn't understand why he asked, nor did I care. I blurted out how I'd lost a check my parents had sent me for a tuition payment and feared telling them. I explained how my car had developed some kind of problem and I didn't know how I was going to get to the small church out in the country where I was supposed to preach next Sunday. I told him about the intense argument with my roommate and how I couldn't live with him any longer. I don't know how long I talked, but it seemed like forever. One frustration, problem, or crisis after another spilled from me.

" 'And all this happened within the last six or seven days?' Dr. Barclay asked. 'Yeah,' I replied. 'It really has been one of the worst weeks of my life.'

"Ever the patient teacher, Dr. Barclay leaned back in his swivel chair and started explaining things about the human body. He told me how we all have this 'fight or flight' reaction and that whenever we're faced with anything we perceive as threatening, our body produces adrenaline to prepare us to either battle (fight) the threat or run (flight) as fast as we can to get away from it. Of course, most of the situations faced by modern humans require neither reaction, but the adrenaline floods our bodies just the same.

" 'The bad thing for you, Joe, is that the adrenaline doesn't dissipate immediately. It takes a while for it to be absorbed back into the body. If another situation you perceive as threatening comes about, it pumps more adrenaline into the system. Of course, that new batch takes a while to go away. If another situation comes along, more adrenaline is produced. After a while, you're literally a walking time bomb. Your body is ready to run or fight, and your nerves are on edge. All it takes is the right trigger, and all that energy explodes.

" 'For example, you weren't really that mad at Gordon, were you?'

"Of course, he was right. Gordon had just said something that didn't sit well, and before I knew what was happening, I was in his face—even though he's twice my size—begging for a fight by verbally trashing him. Dr. Barclay nodded his head in understanding and said, 'I won't file proceedings against you and will forget the whole thing if you do exactly what I tell you to do. Today's Friday. Skip your classes the rest of the day. Send word to the little church in the country that you're sorry but a problem has come up and you can't come. Go to your dorm room and don't come out except to run once each day and to go to the church on the edge of the campus on Sunday morning. Don't even go to the cafeteria to eat. Ask your girlfriend to get sandwiches to you. And when you run, I want you to run until you drop— once each day and alone. Besides that, I want you to sleep, pray, and meditate all weekend and give your body a chance to either use up or absorb some of this stuff. Come back to classes Monday morning, and if you act civil, this is over.' "

All that happened more than thirty years ago when Joe Beam attended a small Christian college. His subsequent ministry to millions of people around the world would never have happened had he been expelled from that college. To this day, he appreciates the wisdom of the perceptive Dr. Barclay. Obviously, that scholarly man knew what some people are just discovering about stress and crises.

THE GREAT GRAY KILLER

You might have seen the poster of a zebra whose rear haunch and leg stripes have come unraveled. As the zebra stands with its stripes curled around its feet like ribbons, the caption notes, "It must be STRESS."

We've all felt like that zebra—as if our stripes are falling off. Maybe you've had experiences similar to the ones described below.

My son wrecked his truck for the third time in about four months. Thankfully, he was not hurt. He had just gotten the truck fixed from the second accident, and now it is back in the shop. He'll have to borrow a car from his brother, or I'll have to take him to work. Plus his insurance will probably be cancelled.

We've been overdrawn at the bank for the last several months. Our expenses have just been larger than usual—no major calamities. We aren't at the point of bankruptcy, but getting our budget back on course is a challenge.

I love the winter holiday season, but I sometimes wish it could be more serene. Everyone has parties, and there are gifts to buy and wrap and special foods to prepare. I get worn out before it's over, and that's too bad.

These are only a few examples. Each of you could add to the list. Stress comes in many shapes and sizes, and each of us experiences stress on a daily basis.

Stress is not new, but our understanding of it has grown in recent years. Dr. Barclay had it right: Our ancestor who encountered a bear or lion while foraging for food experienced stress. Adrenaline flooded his body, his blood pressure surged, and his heart beat faster. He was ready to run faster or fight better as a result. Those same reactions take place in our bodies today when we are stuck in a traffic jam or the boss snarls or a deadline draws near. Unfortunately, those situations don't require fight or flight, and so we experience the strong physical and emotional reactions to stress without an effective way of releasing them.

After months or years of such distress, we feel the effects. Medical science has much evidence that the accumulated effects of stress are important factors in heart disease, angina, arrhythmia, hypertension, migraine headaches, ulcers, diabetes, and many other diseases.

Because stress is a daily part of life, we tend to ignore its serious consequences. Stress takes its toll in subtle but deadly ways—that's why we call it the Great Gray Killer.

The bad news is that stress can kill us, it's with us every day, and we can't get away from it. The good news is that we don't have to suc-cumb to stress—we can take action to manage it. Strong families have discovered some important insights into dealing with stress that have proved successful for them.

Six Tactics for Coping with Stress

TACTIC #1—KEEP THINGS IN PERSPECTIVE

One of the most important things strong families do to minimize stress is to keep things in perspective and realize that stress is a normal part of life. James Taylor sings that everybody gets the blues, and strong families would agree. One man's comment reflects what several said.

Everyone has difficult times. Who doesn't have days when you get a parking ticket, the boss is cross, traffic snarls, the neighbor's dog gets in your trash cans, it rains, and the washing machine blows up? I try to remember that I have plenty of company in misery. That helps me get through.

Knowing we aren't alone or unique gives us courage and a little more enthusiasm for tackling our troubles head-on. Sometimes, thinking of others helps us realize that our problems aren't so big.

One day I was feeling really pressed and depressed. We had guests coming for dinner, the house was messy, and I resented having to cook and clean. As I washed dishes, I suddenly remembered a young woman we knew. She was gravely ill and too weak to get out of bed. We knew she didn't have long to live. The idea flashed in my mind, What would Annette give to have this "awful" day of mine? How happy she'd feel to be able to be up cooking and cleaning or any number of ordinary things.

There's an old adage that says, "It's not the great storm that destroys the giant oak tree—it's the little bugs!" It's ironic that we weather the great storms and crises in life and then allow insignificant, trifling irritations to destroy our happiness and health. One wife explained:

M*y husband and I got trapped in a 3pattern of misunderstanding awhile back. We'd decide to go out for dinner, for fun and relaxation. There we'd be in the car, dressed, hungry, and ready to go. He'd say, "Where shall we eat?" and I'd say, "It doesn't matter," and things would go downhill from there. I couldn't figure out why he was so hostile when I was just trying to be agreeable. He couldn't understand why I was making him guess what I wanted.*

We have a very sound marriage, but this trifle got out of control. Soon it carried over into other conversations such as, "Where shall we vacation?" Every decision ended in a fight.

After one especially angry blowup, we had a long talk and discovered it was all a dumb misunderstanding. "It doesn't matter" was my way of trying to be agreeable, but he resented having to make another decision, which is why he got so angry. He makes decisions all day at work and may be reprimanded if they are "wrong."

So now I make a suggestion when he asks where or what. Sometimes I'll plan the evening and say, "Come on. We're going out, and it's a surprise." I pick the restaurant and maybe plan a play or movie after. He enjoys the surprise and not having to choose.

Other strong family members agree that petty irritants should be recognized as petty and some are best ignored. The spouse who makes a thoughtless remark may have had a bad day at work. Children who don't clean their rooms aren't trying to be mean to their parents; they're just being normal children. The neighbor who doesn't return your wave may not have seen you. Not all irritants are worth confronting.

But some trivialities are difficult to ignore. What about slurping coffee or mannerisms that drive you crazy or something that hurts your feelings? Strong families gave sensible advice.

Iron it out as soon as possible. Be nice. Say, "It really drives me nuts when you crack your knuckles. I know it isn't a big thing; you're a fine person with few flaws." You'll both have a laugh and clear it up.

Don't let resentment build up. Don't pile misunderstanding and hurt on top of misunderstanding and hurt. Get it out in the open. Ask the person who hurt your feelings what was meant. You may discover you misunderstood the action or words. If not, forgive them and go on to other things. Life is too short.

TACTIC #2—LET GO AND LET GOD

One highly successful oil man from Oklahoma, a member of a strong family, summarized the responses of many other strong families when he said:

I used to worry quite a lot; in my business it's easy to do. It got to the point where it was about to break me. Then a very important thing happened to me, and I don't know exactly how: I finally realized deep within myself that it was not possible for me to control every little aspect of my life and the lives of others—as I had been trying to do.

I decided that I should do the best I could do and then let go. I had to trust more in other people and in life. "For none of us lives to himself alone and none of us dies to himself alone."[1] I can't do everything on my own; I can't carry the world on my shoulders. This realization gave me an indescribable feeling of relief.

Worry has been likened to a rocking chair: You make a lot of motion but don't go anywhere. Worry depletes energy, keeps us fearful, and interferes with our effective functioning. One woman shared:

I used to go through two routines: what if and if only.

"If only I hadn't said..." "If only I had..." "If only I were..." "What if it (rains, snows, freezes, is too hot)?" "What if it won't work?" "What if they hate me?"

And on and on and on. I was always miserable.

A friend suggested I write down a list of worries each week. Then I could sketch out what to do about each. I liked that approach, but the real shock came when I looked back at my list several months later. Many were things in the past I couldn't change, and some were things in the present I couldn't control, like whether it rained. I decided I'm too smart to waste so much effort needlessly.

It sounds like this lady learned the two truths of Philippians 4: Turn everything over to God and think only about the good things.

> Do not be anxious about anything, but in everything, by prayer and petition, with thanksgiving, present your requests to God. And the peace of God, which transcends all understanding, will guard your hearts and your minds in Christ Jesus.
>
> Finally, brothers, whatever is true, whatever is noble, whatever is right, whatever is pure, whatever is lovely, whatever is admirable—if anything is excellent or praiseworthy—think about such things.[2]

TACTIC #3—FOCUS ON SOMETHING BIGGER THAN SELF

Having a mission, goal, or being caught up in something larger than ourselves gives us security, confidence, and serenity to deal with the stresses of our daily lives. This was demonstrated so well by strong families. The sense of purpose expressed among strong families revolved around their spiritual beliefs and their concern for each other.

Sometimes in the scrambled schedule of life, I get to feeling that the time I spend with my sons could better be spent on work. And then I remind myself that the budget request or schedule of who works when or the productivity report will affect life for a few days or weeks. I have to do it and it's important, but my job as a father is most important. If I'm a good father to my sons, they'll likely be good parents too. Someday— after I'm gone, and certainly after those reports have rotted—a grand- child or great-grandchild of mine will have a good father because I was a good father. It's kind of a chain reaction.

The secret to not being overwhelmed is to see the daily challenges and frustrations as contributing to something larger. Keep the big picture in mind. See those PTA meetings as improving the school; see your volun- teer hours as easing someone's misery; see the work of caring for your family as creating healthy, productive people who'll make the world a better place.

TACTIC #4—HUMOR YOURSELF

Many people in strong families prescribed humor as an antidote for stress. "Learn to laugh at the crazy things that happen and at yourself," they suggested.

I'm a true fan of M*A*S*H. *We get the reruns every evening. I have some of the episodes memorized and enjoy them all. There's always something that strikes me as funny, and I've thought many times about the way the characters use humor to ease the strain. So many of the sit- uations are true to everyday life—not the war part but the problems with other people, the red tape, the weather, loneliness, et cetera.*

We *try to treat things seriously that need it and poke fun at the rest. We often ask ourselves, "Will this be funny later?" and a good many petty irritants are. I'll give you an example.*

We headed out for a company potluck dinner one evening in a bit of a fluster because we were about five minutes late and my husband was supposed to give the invocation. At the trunk, juggling keys and a casse- role, he tipped the dish and spilled hot casserole on his hand and trousers. He dropped it onto the lawn (killing the grass in that spot!) and ran back inside to change clothes.

We raced off and were halfway there when a police officer pulled us over. We had missed a new no-left-turn sign at an intersection. Of course, the officer wanted to see my husband's license, and you know where his wallet was? Right! At home in the other trousers. There we sat explaining spilled casseroles and changed clothes to the officer. She let us go with a warning. No one would have made up a story like ours. We arrived at the dinner, and my husband said, "I'm sorry we're late, but I am very thankful just to be here. Let me tell you why..." His humor changed a blood-pressure-raising series of incidents into a good story.

Another example comes from Susan, a courageous woman who was born with a rare degenerative disease that slowly constricted her body. She spent her time in a wheelchair. At one point, several years ago, she was in danger of dying; her spine had bent so much that she was down to 30 percent of her normal breathing capacity. She was slowly suffocating.

A major and dangerous operation was her only hope: Her back would be cut open from top to bottom, and stainless steel inserts put into each vertebra to help straighten her spine. She would never be able to walk or run, but she would be *alive*.

She joked about being a "bionic woman" and predicted she'd need a whole new wardrobe. Why new clothes? "Because I'll be six-foot-seven with all those metal spacers in me. And think what havoc I'll cause in airport metal detectors!"

Susan's surgery went well. She was able to achieve several goals she had set. Her spirit and humor continued to inspire many people. Unfortunately, the disease cut her life short not long ago.

Susan's strength and attitude were a marvel to all who knew her. When asked, "How can you laugh so much?" She said, "You know what they say—it's either laugh or cry."

And laughter is often the balm we need for the silliness, madness, and ironies of daily life.

Strong families seem instinctively to understand these great truths: "A happy heart makes the face cheerful, but heartache crushes the spirit"[3] and "A cheerful heart is good medicine, but a crushed spirit dries up the bones."[4]

TACTIC #5—TAKE ONE STEP AT A TIME

When Jesus told people not to worry, he said, "Therefore do not worry about tomorrow, for tomorrow will worry about itself. Each day has enough trouble of its own."[5] Another way of phrasing that great truth is that you shouldn't get ahead of yourself but instead just take things one step at a time. Some of the strong families said the same thing in various ways.

I divide my work up into small segments and just work on one segment at a time. I concentrate only on that one thing, and I don't think about the rest of it. That way I don't feel pressured. As a bonus, I have a sense of accomplishment when each segment is done.

Think of it as living in day-tight compartments. If you think about what you have to do in the next week or month, you can be overwhelmed and exhausted. If you concentrate on today only, you can usually manage.

Minimize Fragmentation

Consider the following story. As you read, you may think it's an exaggeration, but it's not; this story is told just as it happened.

The editor of one of the largest newspapers in the nation was very successful in his career. Active in community programs and various philanthropic endeavors, he almost never had an evening at home. He was always involved in a meeting or project. All of his projects were worthy, but all of them together were simply too much. A sad thing happened. He caught the flu because his body's resistance was low from overwork.

He died.

People can literally die from too much fragmentation. Being pulled in so many directions can overwhelm the mind, the emotions, and the body. In such a weakened state, a person becomes more susceptible to the things that lie in wait to destroy. And just as a person can die from the weaknesses that result from fragmentation, so can families. Just as there are forces lurking to attack the human body (viruses, bacteria, and the like), there are forces in this world that attack families. Strong families withstand them just as strong bodies resist most invading germs. But weak families—like weak bodies—can be destroyed by negative influences and encounters.

We must make sure that fragmentation doesn't weaken our families by pulling us in too many directions at once.

Perhaps the most important way we can deal with the frantic pace of life is to reduce our number of involvements. We can do what our good families do. You recall that they repeatedly told us that they dealt with the hectic pace of life by scratching some activities off their lists, by clearing their calendars, by learning to say no.

Prioritize

Another way strong families deal with the stress of too much to do and too many demands is to set priorities and simplify. Sandra, from Kentucky, was in the process of reworking priorities and simplifying life when she was interviewd. She works at an office and had been rushing home at 5:30 to prepare an elaborate dinner for her husband and teenage sons. After dinner she would do dishes and laundry and tidy the house. She also would scream at the boys and have headaches and muscle spasms.

Sandra made some changes. Dinner is now simpler—soup or something in the slow cooker that can be ready when she comes home. She found that teens can cook simple meals, too, and enjoy helping. They can also be responsible for their own laundry. Her husband helps with dishes, takes out the trash, and vacuums. By deciding that her health and sanity were a higher priority than doing everything for her family and by simplifying the menu and chores, Sandra is practicing good stress management.

TACTIC #6—REFRESH AND RESTORE

A very few exceptional people seem to be able to go at a break-neck pace over a long period of time. These are folks who thoroughly enjoy their work. Consequently, their work is as play to them; it does refresh them. Most of us are not so fortunate. Too much work, worry, stress, hassle, and confusion, and we succumb to burnout.

We all need to restore our minds, spirits, and bodies. Even God rested after the first six days of creation: "By the seventh day God had finished the work he had been doing; so on the seventh day he rested from all his work. And God blessed the seventh day and made it holy, because on it he rested from all the work of creating that he had done."[6] Throughout the Old Testament, God commanded his people to keep that day a holy and restful day. "For six days work is to be done, but the seventh day is a Sabbath of rest, holy to the LORD."[7]

Although God didn't command people to keep the Sabbath in the New Testament, he made it clear that he wants humankind to rest and find refreshment. It is crucial to our lives.

Strong families find rest and refreshment largely through periodic participation in activities that are pleasant and relaxing.

We like to take what we call "aimless" trips about twice a year. We decide on a general destination not too far away. Then we set out and go as we please. We take state and county roads and drive leisurely. We explore little museums, quaint shops, and roadside markets. We stop early to enjoy a swim at the motel before dinner.

Quilting is my refreshment. I can spend the evening quilting or looking through patterns and fabric, and the tension just goes away. I'll be excited about finishing my current project or looking forward to starting a new pattern.

We square dance one night a week—at least. The kids have a junior dance group in the same building. There are dances on special occasions such as Valentine's Day with clubs from other nearby towns. We socialize with several other couples in our club; sometimes we go out for dessert or snacks after the dance.

I retreat to my workbench when I need to relax. I can absorb myself in some woodworking project for a couple of hours and then face the world again.

Get Outside

Many strong families participate in nature and outdoor activities together. Their outdoor pursuits include going on walks or hikes; camping; bird-watching; going on picnics; visiting zoos, botanical gardens, parks, and nature preserves; fishing; canoeing; photography; and playing outdoor games.

Strong families believe that these outdoor practices are such a powerful antidote to stress that they deserve special consideration. Their comments tell us more.

Being out in nature puts life back in perspective for us. Go out on a clear night and look at the countless stars, and you'll know what is and isn't important. Observe the steady change of the seasons, and you'll learn patience.

One of the real benefits of being out is being away from the telephone, television, stereo, and other distractions. We can concentrate on each other. There's time to listen, plan, comfort, and dream.

Try hiking or backpacking or sailing or biking all day and feel that "good" tired feeling of physical fatigue. So much of our fatigue these days is mental that it actually refreshes us to tire the body and let the mind rest.

Exercise

One of the most powerful neutralizers of stress is exercise. For years the world's most famous psychiatric and mental health clinics have prescribed that up to half of the scheduled time each day be devoted to exercise and physical activities. Psychiatrists and counselors are well aware that exercise helps us release tension and get rid of pent-up frustration. The fatigue produced by exercise is, without a doubt, the best and safest tranquilizer.

Many people from good families indicate that they regularly participate in some form of exercise. The families are varied in terms of general health, age, and interests, so the specific forms of exercise vary as well. Bicycling, walking, golf, tennis, canoeing, swimming, skiing, jogging, and working out at a gym were all mentioned.

One executive summed up the benefit of exercise:

I shed tension when I work out with weights. Something about tensing the muscles to lift or push makes the emotional tension release. Plus I feel stronger physically and better about myself, so naturally I am uplifted emotionally too.

Enjoy Pets

Bruce Max Feldmann, a prominent veterinary educator, has observed that pets are unique therapists and help millions of people to cope better with life. They contribute to our emotional well-being, allowing us to love and feel love.

The unconditional love and affection given by pets—especially dogs and cats—are often mentioned as a source of comfort. One Arkansas man said,

I take my old dog out to the creek when I feel sad or stretched too thin. We have a long walk and find a log or rock, and then we sit down and have a talk. I can rant and rave, and he listens. Pure love shines in his eyes.

A Connecticut woman talked about her cat:

This cat of mine never sleeps on the bed with me. She prefers a chair in the dining room. Unless I am sick, and then she comes and sleeps on my feet. Don't ask me how she knows I have a cold or the flu; I guess it's a sixth sense. She's there to comfort me and take care of me the only way she can.

MANAGING THE INEVITABLE

Paul Harvey often points out on his news broadcasts that "you can run, but you can't hide." Some things are inescapable. Daily life brings the strain of deadlines, pressures, irritations, frustrations, demands, and hurts. Living brings change: a new baby, a new job, moving to another house or town, a divorce, a wedding, a promotion, children moving out of the home, retirement.

Experts in stress management tell us that we are wrong to view stress as all bad. After all, a certain amount of tension may improve our performance on many tasks. It's not uncommon for a highly favored sports team to be upset by a less talented team because the players were "flat"—no emotion, no tension, no excitement.

The good families studied have learned to manage the level of stress in their everyday lives. They can't eliminate it any more than you can, but they don't allow it to deplete their reserves of energy and emotion.

Thus far, this chapter has focused on the stress and strain of everyday life. But sometimes life brings major upheavals: serious illness, death, unemployment, fire, divorce, flood, marital infidelity, earthquake, or bankruptcy, to name a few. What about these more disruptive events—these crises?

A DEADLY GAME

It was a good basketball game. Exciting and fast paced. Well, as fast paced as you could expect for a group of university professors. This was just one of many pleasures Richard enjoyed in his life at the university. He ran up and down the court with no serious concerns on his mind. Life was good: He loved teaching, his family was close and happy, he was robust and satisfied.

Then it happened.

As one of his teammates shot the ball, Richard prepared to rebound. But because he had turned his back, he did not see the opposing player who also leaped for the ball. They came down hard, the opposing player's elbow digging into Richard's lower back.

His back hurt and was sore for several days. Richard wasn't worried; he'd had athletic injuries before and expected as much. But the soreness became worse. The pain became excruciating; dizziness, weakness, and nausea plagued him. A long series of medical tests and hospital visits followed. Finally the diagnosis came: a rare disease of the pancreas, triggered by the blow to the back.

"I thought knowing what the problem was would help us treat it," said Richard. "What a mistake that was! I learned my condition was disabling and practically always terminal. Life expectancy was less than two years. And most doctors had never seen the condition in practice, so they didn't know what to do with me."

Richard and his wife, Emily, felt as if their world had come to a sudden stop. Their emotions ran the gamut. Total disbelief. Denial. Anger. Deep depression. Piercing fear. What would this do to their lives? How would it influence their three small children? What would they do? What *could* they do?

The first thing they did was to find the very best medical help available for this disease. That took them to the Mayo Clinic. Although Richard received the best medical care, including the latest treatments, the prognosis was no better. One physician told him, "We're doing all that we possibly can do. But your hope really rests with God."

A devout church member, Richard began to pray as never before. "I prayed several times a day," he said. "I flooded my mind with passages from the Bible. I read them and meditated on their meaning. Luke 18:27 was a favorite: 'The things which are impossible with men are possible with God' [NKJV]."

Daily life was a struggle for Richard and his family for the next six years. Three times he had major surgery; twice he almost died. He was hospitalized repeatedly for infections, pneumonia, liver failure, and reactions to medication. Scarcely a month passed without a hospital stay.

Pain was a constant companion, frequently so bad he could not sleep for days. The removal of his pancreas induced diabetes and caused a total metabolic upheaval. He had digestive disturbances and difficulty regulating his blood-sugar levels.

Naturally, he could not continue a normal work schedule; the university dismissed him. Disability payments were only about half of what his salary had been, so Emily opened a childcare center in their home. That way she could care for her own children and Richard while she supplemented their income.

Still the financial burden was staggering. Hospital bills were enormous; Richard required costly medication on a constant basis. They made repeated trips to the Mayo Clinic. Emily recalled, "People would talk about how fortunate we were to have medical insurance that paid 80 percent of our bills. And that is fortunate, but they didn't stop to think that we had to pay the 20 percent. Twenty percent of one hundred thousand dollars is a large chunk of money; Richard's bills were several times one hundred thousand dollars!"

It has been about twenty-three years since Richard played that fateful basketball game. According to the best medical thought, he should have been dead for over two decades. No one would have been surprised if he and Emily had divorced and the children had run amok! Many would not have predicted their survival through such a long-term crisis. And yet Richard is alive and has improved enough that he can work for short periods of time. He is happy and enthusiastic about life. The relationship between him and his children is close and loving. The children are fine young adults; two have graduated from college. Richard and Emily have a very solid marriage. She has moved on to a better-paying job. All of their problems are not over. In a sense, they never will be; life doesn't work that way. But they do know they can face whatever comes along.

Six Strategies for Surviving a Crisis

The family-strengths research has identified six strategies used by strong families in crisis situations. Of course, not every family in a crisis will use all six, but in general, these are the kinds of actions taken by good families.

STRATEGY #1—SEE THE ROSES AMONG THE THORNS

A primary factor in the survival of strong families is their ability to see something positive in the situation and to focus on that positive element. Richard talked about this:

Emily and the children kept my spirits up and probably prevented me from madness by regularly calling attention to our blessings. No matter how bad we felt, at each meal we all would mention one thing we were really thankful for and appreciated about our life together. I remember one day our six-year-old said something that had enormous impact on me.

He said, "I am so happy Daddy is with us more now than he used to be." I thought, well, this is an opportunity to spend time with the children. Why not feel good about it and take advantage of it?

Could that be the thought in Philippians 4 when we are told that instead of being anxious we should pray with *thanksgiving?*[8]

Paul and Carol in Portland, Oregon, are good examples too. Paul has a congenital inner-ear problem that affects his hearing and his balance. At first, Paul was only embarrassed by his out-of-whack balance mechanisms. Speaking in front of large audiences in his job as an educator for the county schools, he often felt queasy and dizzy. He worried about stumbling. Embarrassment turned to fear when, while driving to work one morning, the vertigo came without warning. The street tumbled over and over on itself, and he crashed into a barricade in a grocery parking lot.

A year and two operations later, the prognosis was still unclear. He might need more surgery; he might never be better. The doctors were not hazarding a guess at this juncture. But before this crisis could be resolved, another one hit the family. Hard.

Budget cuts were made in their county school system: Paul was out of a job. Twice he had earned outstanding educator awards in his state. Now he would be walking the pavement looking for work; if, that is, he could walk in spite of the vertigo.

Paul and Carol no doubt spent some time bemoaning their fate. But they ended up reframing the situation.

When asked if he was depressed, he said,

Nope. This may sound silly, but as Carol says, it's a good time to move on. I've been in education twenty years, and this will be the impetus to get out of my rut and try something new.

I'm not sure what I'll do. A blind man down the street became a millionaire selling Tupperware or something over the phone. I won't sell Tupperware, but I have been selling education for twenty years. I've been operating on my mouth. I will continue.

Carol is really getting into her career. She is doing a bang-up job for the church now. She's chartered a plane to fly a group to the state meeting that she put together. In twenty years in education, I never got to charter a plane!

We are stronger now than ever. This is about the worst thing that has happened to us in twenty-one years of marriage. And yet we really love each other, and the kids are pulling together with us like never before. We are all in this together. We are going to make it.

Now please don't get the wrong idea here. No one's suggesting that we should be naive fools merrily dancing a jig while the world goes up in flames. Nor are people in strong families unrealistic Pollyannas who are never knocked down by tragedy: They cry, get angry, feel hurt, and are depressed. But they are not overwhelmed by crisis and tragedy—partly because they manage to see some good in bad situations. Their ability to do this helps them maintain a more balanced perspective; it prevents them from becoming so depressed and despondent that they cannot function.

It's much like the thought of Romans 8:28: "And we know that in all things God works for the good of those who love him, who have been called according to his purpose."

In other words, the ability to see something good in a bad situation gives strong families hope!

My brother died suddenly last fall; he was forty-three. After the initial shock and grief, I did some looking into my own life. I guess you could say I asked myself, "What if I only make it to forty-three?" I've made some financial arrangements so that my young children are better protected if I die early, and I feel good about that. I also have a renewed appreciation for how precious each day of life is. I try not to waste a single day.

I don't recommend that you burn the house to learn this lesson, but our family did stand together in our front lawn one frosty fall morning and look at the pile of ashes that had been our home. And then we looked at each other, and suddenly we were hugging and crying with joy because we were okay. And we are what is most important to each other.

When my family broke apart, I thought I was going to lose my mind. That's the lowest I've ever been; it was terrible—indescribable. Today, four years later, I'm alive. My ex-wife and I still don't speak much, but the kids like me, and my parents see that it wasn't all my fault. Some, but not all. And one really good thing came of it. I learned that being at rock bottom at least once in your life is useful in the long run. It gives you something to gauge your life against. Now when bad things happen, I can think back and say to myself, "This is bad, but nothing compared to the way it was."

The hard times in our lives have taught us things about ourselves. Folk wisdom reminds us that a catastrophe that doesn't kill you will make you stronger. We've learned that we are tough and strong—real survivors.

There's a poster that sums up what we've been talking about. It says:
> Roses have thorns or
> Thorns have roses.
> How do you see life?

STRATEGY #2—PULL TOGETHER

Members of strong families unite to face the challenges of a crisis. They don't insincerely ask, "What needs to be done?" Instead, they sincerely ask, "What can I do?" Sometimes the task is enormous. Nobody could do it alone. Strong family members focus on the small things they can do as individuals. No individual feels total responsibility for the problem. Nobody carries the load alone. They shoulder it together.

Emily and Carol, as mentioned earlier, took jobs to ease financial burdens. Children may help with household chores, yard work, or answering the phone. Each family member is a support—physically and emotionally—to the others. Some examples help to show how this works.

Pat received a significant promotion several months ago. It made her the woman with the highest management-level position in her company, and she regarded it with mixed emotions. She was delighted to advance but felt tremendous pressure to do well, not only for herself but for the other female employees.

This promotion was a crisis because it required a dramatic change in her lifestyle. Her husband, Ed, and their teen daughter, Becky, pitched in to help. Becky agreed to handle laundry and kitchen cleanup to give Mom time to do reports at home.

"Ed has been a sounding board for ideas and has been my 'counselor' when I needed to pour out fears and anxieties. Just someone to listen is so important," said Pat.

Ed laughed. "Yes, and I started something I could hardly afford. At the end of her first week in the new position I sent her a single rose; the next week I sent two as a way of saying, 'You made it another week.' When we got to a dozen, we agreed to quit. She felt confident enough not to need that extra little pat on the back. Maybe I should have picked cheaper flowers, huh?"

Jeff and Linda bought a lovely home near a little creek. As far as anyone knew, the creek had never been out of its banks. Last summer their town received six inches of rain in two hours. The floodwaters were four feet deep in their living room. Neither was hurt, but they lost all their furniture and appliances, and many personal belongings were ruined. Both of their families helped them. Her parents, who live nearby, gave them a place to stay. His brother and sister gave them muscle and time to clean up mud and trash. Dens, basements, and attics have yielded "extras": a bed, a table, a refrigerator, chairs, lamps, and linens. Because the family members pulled together, Jeff and Linda made it through this difficult time.

Other families told how they joined in to help each other during crises.

*A*while ago we were moving as a result of a job transfer. My sister came to help us pack. We couldn't have made it without her. If she hadn't come, I'd still be there packing boxes!

*S*everal years ago, my mother was dying after a long and courageous battle with cancer. She was confined to bed and needed lots of care. Our adult daughter came home to help out. She helped with nursing chores and tough decisions—like should we put Mom in a nursing home?—and with tedious details, such as figuring out Medicare and health insurance claims.

*M*y brother helped pull me through a serious illness several years ago. He's not a physician, but he gave me medicine for my spirit. We're from Texas, and you know how proud Texans are just to be Texans. He said to me over and over, "Jim, you're just like a Texas longhorn— mean and tough and not too pretty. You know, longhorns aren't much to look at, but they are noted for being tough, and they survive where other cattle cannot." Soon I found myself thinking, "Yeah, I'm tough."

STRATEGY #3—GO GET HELP

Family members—spouses, children, parents, siblings—provide much of the help that a family needs to make it through a crisis. Fortunately, most families don't have to make it alone. And strong families are smart enough to seek out valuable support from others— their church, friends, neighbors, and professionals.

Richard and Emily received much assistance from their church, friends, and neighbors. Countless hours of childcare were given by friends and neighbors during Richard's many hospital visits so that Emily could be with him. Food was brought in during difficult times. Their congregation bought airline tickets for one of their trips to the Mayo Clinic and arranged for Emily to stay with a family in Rochester during Richard's hospitalization there. An "anonymous friend" paid the tuition so their son could continue his music lessons. Other members of strong families share how vital help from others can be.

*T*hree friends were particularly helpful to me following the death of my wife. One lady came to the house immediately; she tidied up the living room and cleaned the refrigerator because she knew people would be coming to visit and bringing food. Then she fixed the guest room because she knew some relatives from out of town would be coming. She stayed at the house all day taking calls, keeping a record of who brought what so I could write thank-you notes later. She made coffee for the friends who dropped by to pay their respects. I was in no shape to handle all that plus the funeral arrangements.

Her husband picked up my relatives at the airport and later drove them to the funeral home. They both provided long-term support by visiting me, having me in their home, and showing they were concerned.

The third friend is an older lady, a widow. She went with me to make funeral arrangements and to select a cemetery lot. She, too, was there when I needed her for years after my wife's death.

*M*y wife was cleaning out closets and passing on outgrown clothes to the Goodwill box when she found a packet of marijuana and a pipe in our teen daughter's closet. We were horrified and frightened. As soon as we collected our wits, we realized we weren't equipped to handle this alone.

We talked with our family attorney, and she gave us a copy of our state's laws about drug possession. We talked with a drug rehabilitation counselor who gave us information about symptoms of addiction; he recommended two or three courses of treatment, depending on how serious our daughter's involvement was.

We had done our homework when we confronted our daughter a few days later. We had solid information about the legal and physical danger she was in. We didn't have any trouble conveying our deep concerns for her, and I think she responded to that better than she would have to our initial shock and fear.

*T*he worst crisis I've come through was the breakup of my first marriage. I had been lulled into thinking my spouse was as perfectly content as I. When he came home one night muttering something vague about *"needing a change, needing to grow, needing to be free,"* I reacted with disbelief. It sounded too much like a soap opera.

His malaise never dissipated, though, and in a month he was gone. He never came back. There I was with four small children, no job, and not much education. I cried for about three solid days. Then some friends began to help me pick up the pieces.

My closest friend volunteered to keep the children while I went job hunting. Another, who had just begun job hunting herself, gave me tips on interviewing and writing a résumé. Our neighbor who teaches at the university talked with me about the possibility of going to college. He brought me a catalog and enrollment forms.

I have a network of five friends who counsel and console me. If one is not at home, I call another. Two of them are professionals: one at the university and one at the community mental health center. But they all help me. And if I have a really rough problem, I call four or five of them in a row. I tell my sad story, they listen and offer suggestions, and then I make a decision.

STRATEGY #4—USE SPIRITUAL RESOURCES

In the previous chapter we learned about the spiritual dimension in the lives of strong families and how important it is to them. It is not surprising, then, that they draw on those spiritual resources in times of crises, just as they draw on the physical resources of energy and muscle and the emotional resources of family commitment and concern. Many find their faith in God's help and guidance to be a powerful force in dealing with crises.

Take time to read the eleventh chapter of the book of Hebrews sometime. In it, you'll find story after story of men and women who persevered through one crisis after another. Their ability to make it through came totally from their faith in God and his truthfulness. That chapter begins with these words: "Now faith is being sure of what we hope for and certain of what we do not see."

In times of crises, spiritual beliefs provide a philosophy of life, perspective, hope, and comfort. Members of strong families shared their beliefs.

When our business went bankrupt, we were faced with losing our whole way of life. Financial fear tore us apart. But a turning point for us was when we rediscovered God's promise in the book of Isaiah: "So do not fear, for I am with you; do not be dismayed, for I am your God. I will strengthen you and help you; I will uphold you with my righteous right hand."[9]

We remembered that God was with us and would help us through this difficult time. In our prayers we committed our situation into God's hands and thanked him for giving us divine guidance and protection. We felt a confidence and a peace about everything. We came through the situation well, and our bonds with each other and with God became stronger.

A few years ago, we were living in a large urban area. It was not a good place to rear our children. The lifestyle was very materialistic and hectic; it was too crowded. My husband's job, though it carried a high salary, was very stressful and not satisfying. It left him with too little time for the family. In short, we were miserable.

We prayed about this for some time, and we had many serious conversations about what we could do. Finally, we came to the decision that we would leave. That may not sound earth shaking, except that we made that decision without knowing where we would go or if we could find a job somewhere else. We asked God to guide and help us, and we had faith that he would. It may sound strange, but we did not worry about it.

About one week after we made that decision, a job offer came. It was a good offer, the kind of work my husband wanted, and in our number one choice of places to live. And my husband hadn't even applied for it—didn't realize the opening was there. The company representative who called him said they were hoping that he would be interested in the job but didn't know if they could lure him away from where he was. (Little did they know!)

We put our house on the market, and it sold ten days later. We located a truck rental company that had a special offer that was about *half what others were charging. A minister friend drove two thousand miles to help us move. He said that all ministers know how to pack and move. We couldn't have done it without him.*

In two months' time, we made our decision to leave, had a job offer, sold our house, packed the truck, and left for our new home and life. We know that only God could have put all these things in place. It wasn't luck, and it wasn't circumstance. It was God. We continue to marvel at how it all happened, and we praise God for this obvious blessing in our lives.

STRATEGY #5—OPEN CHANNELS OF COMMUNICATION

When five-year-old Elizabeth developed a puzzling kidney problem, her parents, Quinzola and Raymond, were terrified. "We didn't know what to do," Raymond explained. "We were working closely with the doctors, and all they could say was that exploratory surgery would have to be performed. Perhaps in surgery they could find out exactly what was happening."

The surgery was set for mid-May—eight weeks away. For several weeks, Elizabeth was the unsuspected sufferer in this family in crisis. Quinzola and Raymond felt inadequate to tell Elizabeth anything except that she would have an operation. Raymond explained,

I rationalized the whole situation away for a while. I convinced myself that I should wait until I had better information before I talked with Elizabeth. Or I told myself that she's only five and this is passing over her anyway.

All my rationalizing was wrong, of course. Elizabeth proved that to us soon enough. Quinzola overheard Elizabeth and her eight-year-old sister, Anna, talking about school in the fall. Anna had said, "Oh, Elizabeth, you'll love Mrs. Palmer. She's so good. She's my favorite teacher at Calvin School."

And Elizabeth was grumpy and said, "No, I won't."

Anna persisted, "Oh, you will. Mrs. Palmer is great. You'll love her."

"No, I won't!"

"Why not?"

"Because I'll be dead!"

Quinzola and I felt terrible. Elizabeth was worrying and suffering all alone because we were too afraid to help her. We agreed I would talk with her. Later that evening I sat in my favorite rocker with Elizabeth on my lap. I said, "Elizabeth, you're going to have an operation in a few weeks. Do you know what the doctors are going to do?"

"No, Daddy."

Being an electrical engineer, I know how to diagram things, so I took out my trusty number two pencil and a piece of paper and drew a diagram of kidneys, urethras, and a bladder. I explained exploratory surgery.

But I knew there was something more important. So I forged bravely on, "Elizabeth, you know that sometimes people—even little kids—die during an operation. But not very often at all, especially when they're healthy. And you're healthy. The doctors tell us that you should be fine, and Mommy and I will do everything we can so the operation will be a success and you won't hurt. The doctors say you need to have this operation or your kidney could get worse and worse, and that would be very bad for you."

Raymond finished his story, explaining that he and Quinzola probably drove the doctors to distraction asking for explanations and assurances. "But she's our daughter!" he exclaimed.

The operation was a success. Elizabeth's kidneys were repaired, and she is eighteen years old today and as healthy as can be. "The only thing we couldn't take care of completely was the pain—she was a sore little kid for several days after the surgery."

Rabbi Earl Grollman in Belmont, Massachusetts, said that children can easily become the "lost souls in a family in crisis." What he means is that when families are stricken by tragedy, the adults sometimes are so smothered by their own fear and grief that they cannot attend to the needs of the children. He advises that the adults in the family force themselves to think about how the children feel.

A valuable benefit of open communication is that it allows family members to express feelings freely. Crises are times of change and uncertainty; people caught up in them may feel loss, anger, fear, anxiety, and guilt. Being able to express these feelings is a step toward surviving the crisis.

One young man interviewed is an accomplished pilot. He had become concerned when his father—a high-powered, go-go-go, Type-A personality lawyer—decided to learn to fly to make professional travel easier.

Dad took a few lessons and was certified competent. But I had my doubts; in fact, I was scared when I went up with him. But he was always too expert, too professional, too cool around me. I couldn't argue with him. So I made a joke: "If you are going to fly, you'd better get a lot of insurance, because you're terrible. You're going to kill yourself. Ha. Ha. Ha."

Some joke. A few weeks later he went out to practice his new skills. I wanted to go up with him because he was so awful, but my wife and I had planned to go to Sioux Falls to visit her sister's family. We hadn't seen them in several years.

It happened. Dad crashed and was killed instantly.

For some time I was obsessed with guilt and anger: anger at him for going; guilt that I didn't go with him. I had to talk with someone because I couldn't handle it alone. I told my wife what I was feeling; told my brother too.

My wife said time after time, "You didn't know what was going to happen. He was certified to fly, so someone thought he was okay in the air. It was his decision to fly—not yours!"

My brother told me to ease off blaming myself. He said, "Dad's always been bullheaded. And he was a grown man capable of making choices. If he chose not to listen to you, that's his fault. I love him as much as you do, but that doesn't change how stubborn he was."

Without their help I would have sunk into a terrible stew of anger, guilt, and depression. And I might not have gotten that help if I hadn't told them how I felt.

Another benefit of opening communication channels is that problem solving is made easier. A mother from Colorado said,

As the time of our youngest daughter's wedding approached, I called a family council. Things were getting out of control. Weddings have a way of growing—more guests, more food, more flowers, more money! We just couldn't afford the size this one was gaining. And I was very nervous about getting all the arrangements made; I was swamped.

Our daughter—the bride-to-be—was relieved to simplify the wedding. We decided to have a less elaborate reception to reduce costs considerably. My husband suggested letting his mother do the flowers. She's done flower arranging for years as a hobby and is quite talented. He also volunteered to line up the photographer and musicians.

Both my husband and daughter were willing to help. They hadn't realized how near an anxiety attack I was. We all felt better to get our plan of attack formulated.

STRATEGY #6—GO WITH THE FLOW

A final characteristic of strong families that allows them to weather the storms of life is their adaptability or flexibility. A proverb tells of the mighty oak, so tall and firm, that breaks in the strong wind while the fragile-looking reeds bend to the ground but do not snap. Good families tend to be like the reeds. They bend, they change, they adapt, and when the storm is over they're still intact.

Richard learned to cook and clean and operate the washing machine when Emily went to work. "We traded places," he said. "She couldn't do everything, and it made me feel more useful." Emily learned to think of herself as the family breadwinner. Other families told similar stories of men and women learning new tasks and roles, changing careers, or going back to school to train for a job.

One woman spoke about retirement:

We had thought of retirement as a reward for years of hard work. All the hoopla—parties and gifts—leads up to retirement. And then you wake up one morning wondering, Now what?

It didn't take Roger long to catch up on sleeping late and television sports. Soon, he was hanging around watching me do housework. Then he began offering advice, and that was too much for me! I seemed to spend all day puttering around and getting very little done. We were both feeling aimless.

It took some time, but we worked out a style of living that suits us. For one thing, we follow a general schedule. We are not fanatic clock watchers, but we have breakfast around eight and do house and yard chores until lunchtime. We work together on the chores—Roger especially likes to cook. One day a week we go to town: to the bank, post office, grocery, and such.

Afternoons are varied. I volunteer at the hospital two afternoons a week and take a craft class one other day. Roger never had time for volunteer work during his employed years. He has become active in county and state politics; he had a wonderful time working for his favorite candidates during the last elections. In slack times, he enjoys his coin and knife collections.

We visit friends at least one evening a week—either at their homes or in ours, for cards or board games. Roger and I have been able to travel more. We took an extended trip to Australia to visit one of my elderly aunts and her children. We hadn't seen them in many years, and it was wonderful.

We had to decide how to structure our time. We had to adapt to more free time and more time together. We changed the way we divided household chores. If we hadn't been able to make those changes, we'd have been pretty miserable.

A BANK ACCOUNT

As you read through the strategies strong families use to cope with crises, you probably noticed that a couple of them were discussed before. Entire chapters have been devoted to spiritual well-being and communication, and it isn't too hard to see family willingness to pull together as an expression of their commitment to one another.

In short, the strengths of these families serve as a pool of resources that they draw from when times are difficult—rather as we save money for a "rainy day." In contrast, unhealthy families are worn out and depleted on a daily basis by the stress of poor relationships. When a crisis comes along, the unhealthy family must add it to the burden they already struggle to bear. No wonder the extra load is sometimes too much.

A TURNING POINT

The Chinese system of writing uses pictographs to convey meaning. The ancient Chinese symbol for the word *crisis* is a composite of two other symbols: the symbol for *danger* and the symbol for *opportunity*. The implication is clear: While crises undoubtedly bring difficulty and sometimes danger, when viewed positively and creatively, they can be opportunities for personal and family growth. They can be the beginning of better times.

FAMILY
AT
WORK
Putting It to Work—Six Ideas for Your Family

1. *Assess the stress in your life.* To help people measure the stress in their lives, Dr. Thomas Holmes, a psychiatrist, developed the Social Readjustment Rating Scale. This test assigns point values for various stressors. You'll notice that not all the "Events" are negative: Even positive events like getting married or going on vacation are sources of stress because they represent change. To take the test, simply add up the total of all the "Impact" values of all the life "Events" you have experienced in the past year. If you score below 150 points, your stress level isn't very high. You probably aren't experiencing discomfort. If you score between 150 and 300 points, you need to safeguard your health and make an effort to reduce stress. If you score more than 300, you need to be especially careful and take concrete steps to reduce stress.

THE SOCIAL READJUSTMENT RATING SCALE

Event	*Impact*
Death of a spouse	100
Divorce	73
Marital separation	65
Jail term	63
Death of a close family member	63
Personal injury or loss	53
Marriage	50
Fired at work/lost job	47
Marital reconciliation	45
Retirement	45
Change in health of family member	44
Pregnancy	40
Sexual difficulties	39
Gain of new family member	39
Business readjustment	39
Change in financial state	38
Death of a close friend	37
Change to a different line of work	36
Change in number of arguments with spouse	35
Mortgage over $50,000*	31
Foreclosure of mortgage or loan	30
Change in responsibilities at work	29
Son or daughter leaving home	29
Trouble with in-laws	29
Outstanding personal achievement	28

Please remember that these are relative estimates of how stressful a life change usually is. Your circumstances may make any event more (or less) stressful for you. If, for example, both you and your spouse must work full-time to meet car and house payments, "fired at work" might be weighted a 75 rather than a 47, and "pregnancy" might more nearly be a 65 than a 40.

*Holmes original figure was $10,000. We have inflated the figure to make it more realistic. And you may find it a more helpful estimate of the impact of financial stress to consider your total indebtedness.

2. *Commit yourself to an exercise program.* Walking is a generally safe and effective method of exercising, and it's *free.* You might walk or jog three times each week by yourself and play tennis or bicycle with a loved one on weekends.

3. *Cultivate your sense of humor.* Collect Ogden Nash poems or Erma Bombeck or Louis Grizzard books. Make a scrapbook of cartoons you especially enjoy. Buy a Dilbert calendar. Use a VCR to make a collection of your favorite comedy series that you can find in reruns—*Bob Newhart, The Mary Tyler Moore Show, The Carol Burnett Show,* or *I Love Lucy.* Rent or buy a collection of Marks Brothers movies. Whatever you and your family find funny will be a great thing to share on regular occasions.

4. *Select a hobby that refreshes and pleases you.* Many people find it helpful to make their recreation something that contrasts with what they do all day at work. For example, if you read a good deal in your work, select a hobby that is manual—gardening or crafts. If you work with people all day, you might enjoy a solitary activity for fun. (Of course, don't forget the things you do with your family.) If your work is at a desk, pick a hobby that is physically active.

5. *Periodically review plans concerning death.* Consult a lawyer about wills, power-of-attorney documents, and "living wills," and keep them current. Review each other's wishes concerning funerals, memorial services, burial, cremation, and so on. Make sure you both know the location of insurance policies, bank accounts, deeds to property, car titles, and other important papers. Children can be included in these discussions when they are older. Some couples make the review about every five years. They connect it with an event such as someone's birthday or an anniversary to help them remember. Or it can be given its own arbitrary anniversary—June 1 in years ending in 0 or 5 (2000 and 2005, for example). Put it on the calendar, and then celebrate with a nice dinner afterward. Planning such as this does not make you die any sooner; it does help your family when the time comes.

6. *Use television and movies as a catalyst for family discussions.* Consider the crises portrayed in television dramas and the news. Ask your family: "What can this person (family) do? What good can you see in this situation? Who could help? What did this person or family do that helped? Hindered?"

BECOMING A FANTASTIC FAMILY

There was a time when our family situation seemed hopeless. Carl and I had drifted apart. We didn't talk anymore. Because we were head over heels in debt, both Carl and I began to moonlight with second jobs.

"That seemed to make things worse rather than better. Things became more tense, and sometimes the stress was so unbearable, all I wanted to do was run.

"Unfortunately, we took our frustrations out on each other and the kids. We had terrible arguments over trivial things. One night one of these arguments ended with Carl hitting me hard in the face. Oh, he was immediately apologetic and genuinely sorry for what happened. It scared me, but I didn't think it could ever happen again. Three weeks later it did. Only this time he hit me repeatedly. I was hurt so bad I had to go to the hospital. My nose was broken and my jaw was dislocated. I remember lying in that hospital bed thinking there was nothing left to hold our family together. I was in the hospital, the police had Carl, and my kids were with my sister. I mean, what hope could anyone feel in that situation?

"Carl finally worked out some kind of deal with the district attorney's office so that he wouldn't have to serve time if he got the help he needed—and if he didn't do anything like that again.

"I refused to see him or take his calls. He knew better than to try to come home if I didn't want him there. He sent several notes, which I threw away unopened. I decided divorce was the only answer.

"The divorce proceedings progressed over the next several weeks. Strangely, I didn't feel a sense of relief or satisfaction; I felt empty. One day, my Aunt Helen, who has always been particularly close to me, asked what was wrong.

" 'It doesn't feel right,' I replied. 'I thought divorce would be best for everybody. But now, I'm not sure. The children aren't happy. I'm certainly not. And Carl, oh, I don't know.'

" 'Sounds to me like down deep somewhere you want to save your marriage,' Aunt Helen said. 'If that's really what you want, you can't dwell on the past.' She paused for a couple of seconds and then said, 'If you and Carl give it everything you have, maybe you can build your family into what you want it to be.'

" 'But our family is such a terrible failure,' I replied.

" 'You can learn from your failures' was Aunt Helen's sound advice. 'They can be your guides for what to avoid and what to do differently tomorrow.'

"My aunt's words echoed in my thoughts for a long time. I decided one thing—both Carl and I were guilty of extreme neglect of our marriage and family. We had focused our time and attention on work—two jobs each—and making ends meet. And yes, we were also committed to our misery. We were always frustrated, mad, and hassled. Because there was no time for anything else, we just left each other out. I wondered what would happen if we really did commit ourselves to each other and the kids.

"I picked up the phone and called Carl. We talked more openly and honestly than we had done at any time in our marriage. We even cried together. Carl told me he met regularly with a group for abusive men and had been going to their meetings each week. He was so ashamed that he had lost control like that.

"We decided to see our minister, who is also a certified family therapist, and allow him to guide us on when it was safe for Carl to move back into our home. At the minister's suggestion, we made a list of what had been wrong in our marriage and what we wanted to change. We set goals for what we wanted our family to become. And then we developed realistic plans to accomplish those goals.

"One of the first things we did was to quit our second jobs. They were causing too much stress. We sold one of our cars and eliminated an expensive monthly payment. We rented a smaller house. We don't eat out often. I sew my clothes. We don't have any expensive hobbies. It wasn't easy, but we started making ends meet.

"Another goal was to spend more time together as a family. And we wanted it to be pleasant—fun and recreational. In the past, our time together had been everything but pleasant. We were all so tired and irritable that all our efforts were spent on surviving day to day. No wonder our family had not been a happy place to live.

"Our minister encouraged us to remember that we had friends and relatives who were cheering us on and hoping for the best for us. He told us they could help us by being a sort of cheerleading section.

"We began family prayers each evening before dinner. Not just a blessing for the meal. We prayed for ourselves and our family and for other people as well.

"Well, the changes came—slowly, but they came. Two nights each week were fun nights for the family to play cards or rent a video. Or sometimes we went to the mall for craft and antique shows together. We came to know the children in a way we never had before. They really are neat kids. Carl and I rediscovered our love for each other. Now we can't imagine not talking with each other. And sex is better too!

"That turning point was years ago. We still have rough spots and quarrels, but they aren't violent anymore. Over time, our family has evolved into a happy place to be. It took a lot of effort to become a strong family, but it was worth it!"

Ellen, a West Virginia woman, told the story you just read. It begins this chapter for two reasons: The first is that Ellen and Carl's circumstance seemed so dire that most folks would have given up hope for that family. The second is that by the grace of God, they were able to put it all together again and be a happy family.

If they can do it, you can too.

If your family is already fantastic, you can make it even more fantastic.

If your family is just "so-so," you can make it fantastic.

If your family seems hopeless, you can still make it fantastic.

All you need is the love of God and the decision that from this moment on, you will chart your family's destiny to make it all you want it to be.

WILL THESE SIX SECRETS HELP FAMILIES IN TROUBLE?

The power of these six steps to help even families in trouble—families filled with discord and stress, families who feel absolutely hopeless—lies in the answer to the question *Can people really change?* In other words, *Can weak families become strong?*

The answer, of course, is *yes!* People change and learn every day; weak families *do* become strong—so naturally, you can too.

Too often we operate under the false assumption that people who are successful have always been that way. Not so. Did you know that Margaret Mitchell received numerous rejections of her manuscript *Gone with the Wind* and was advised to rewrite it completely? Or were you aware that Albert Einstein, Nobel laureate, didn't pass his college entrance exams?

Just as famous and successful people weren't always famous and successful, so families that are now strong may not have always been that way. Many currently strong families would describe themselves as having been troubled, mediocre, or on the verge of breaking up. Many have overcome communication problems, infidelity, lack of interest, outside demands, alcohol or other drug abuse, or family violence to become the fantastic families they are today. If they can do it, you can too.

SIX ACTION STEPS TO HELP YOU MAKE IT HAPPEN

Now you know what it takes to build a fantastic family. And now it's time to put what you know into action. As you surely know, fantastic families are not built overnight. It takes work and effort and time. But as the families in the strong-families research have said time and time again—the effort is well worth it.

If you are ready to become all you can be as a family, the following six action steps will help get you started.

ACTION STEP #1—ASSESS YOUR FAMILY'S STRENGTHS

Use the tool "Assessing Your Family's Strengths," Appendix A of this book, to gain greater insight into your family. After each family member who is old enough to understand the words (or old enough to have the words explained to them) completes the assessment, share your answers with one another. As you see how each of you views the characteristics listed, you'll get an idea of where your family's strengths are. You'll also gain an awareness of areas requiring growth. Talk about the areas of agreement first. What do you all agree are your family's strengths and weaknesses? Then discuss the areas that received mixed reviews.

The purpose of your family discussion is *not* to convince another family member to change his or her assessment, but to understand why each family member feels the way he or she does. Use this tool with gentleness and understanding. Don't argue about it, and don't use it to hurt feelings. Use it as a tool to identify the strengths already in existence in your family and the strengths that you can develop. Rather than concentrating on the characteristics that are weak or lacking, rejoice in the strengths you already have!

ACTION STEP #2—HAVE A FAMILY DREAM SESSION

After you use the assessment to get a "snapshot" of where you are, the next step is to get every family member to visualize what you want your family to become. Have a "dream" session together where the entire family sits quietly for several minutes visualizing what they want the family to be like. When each person indicates that he or she is ready, have each in turn share his or her "visualization." Make sure that each person's vision is greeted with only warm and accepting comments.

ACTION STEP #3—CHOOSE SPECIFIC GOALS

Now it's time to decide on some goals. While the entire family is still gathered and all dreams have been shared, work out together a list of goals for your family to accomplish. Perhaps someone wants to have more fun times together. Someone else may suggest a movie night where you rent a wholesome movie, make popcorn, and have a discussion of the movie once it's finished. After all goals are listed, have the family come to agreement on the top ten goals and write them on a poster with goal dates beside each goal.

ACTION STEP #4—MAKE A FAMILY-POTENTIAL ACTION PLAN

With goals agreed on and listed, commit to achieving them by making a plan of action. For example, if one of the ten goals is to have more fun together, have a brainstorming session to come up with as many activities as possible that the family would like doing together. Agree on the best choices and make them part of the plan.

Appoint a "family action plan" captain who will make sure that the family participates in the family action plan each week. With the consent and agreement of all, the captain will set times and dates that each person agrees to honor.

ACTION STEP #5—TAKE ADVANTAGE OF OUTSIDE RESOURCES

Probably 95 percent or more of the effort and problem solving needed to become a fantastic family will come exclusively from your family without any outside help. Becoming a stronger family is definitely a do-it-yourself project.

However, we all need reinforcement and encouragment from out-side sources. There are a vast array of church and community helps available. When your church offers a seminar on parenting or mar-riage—sign up! If your youth minister has a series of classes for parents and teens—go! If your community offers seminars or training classes that fit the values of your family—take advantage of them. And if your family's problems are bigger than you can handle alone—don't hesitate to get professional help. Several specific types of resources and how to choose the best ones for your family are discussed in Appendix D.

ACTION STEP #6—COMMIT TO THE PROCESS

Strong families indicated in hundreds of different ways that the effort must be ongoing. Building a strong family is a *process*, not a one-time event. And implementing the six steps outlined in this book takes long-term commitment. It means changing the way you think about your family and the way you prioritize your life.

One of the great things about these six steps is that they all inter-act with each other in dynamic and powerful ways. As you put your family plan into action, you won't see changes in only one area at a time; you'll find that as you improve in one area, other areas will improve as well.

For example, as family members grow in *commitment* to the family, they will spend more *time* with one another. Commitment also enables the family to *pull together* in a crisis and to work at improving *communication*.

Family members who spend pleasant *time together* reinforce *com-mitment* and *communication*.

Expressed appreciation and *affection* reinforce *commitment*.

Good *communication* is necessary in *crises* and in expressing *appreciation*.

Spiritual well-being is central to *coping with stress and crises*, to *appreciating* the value of people, to valuing *time together*, and to being *committed* to each other.

It's all part of the ongoing process.

THE BEST INVESTMENT

The family has been described as the nucleus of civilization and as the natural, fundamental unit of society. And the thousands of strong families in the strong-families research who shared their secrets reinforce this idea. Family is vital and here to stay.

It follows logically, then, that the cost of becoming a strong family isn't too high. The effort and work required to learn new skills and make family our number one priority is significant. Becoming a strong family demands an investment of time, energy, spirit, and heart.

Ellen, from West Virginia, earlier in the chapter said, "It was more than worth the effort." Other strong family members have said the same: The effort is worth it; they don't regret their sacrifices for their families. One woman said, "I look at what I put into my family—my sweat and tears and love and muscle and mind—as an investment in their future, my future, our future. It's the best investment I can make."

THE BEGINNING

A man and his young son walked along the beach. They stopped to gaze out at the endless ocean. "Just think, Joey," said the father, "the waves breaking at our feet have come from far across the sea."

After a few moments of contemplation, Joey observed sadly, "The waves are dying at our feet. They come to the end of their long trip from across the ocean and then they die. This is the end for the waves."

"No," the father replied, "this is not the end. This is the beginning—the beginning of their long journey back across the sea."

From across the vast expanse of this great and good nation as well as other countries around the world, good families have sent their wisdom and insight about building family strengths and enriching relationships. We thank them for their unselfish sharing.

You now have a solid foundation on which to build. With the help of God, you have everything you need to create your own strong family.

And so, as we come to the end of this book, we realize, as Joey's father said, that this is not really the end. This is the beginning of your quest for a stronger, happier family. Your quest can be a blessing not only to you but to the lives of your children and your children's children. The ripple effect of your efforts today will extend far into the future.

May God bless you as you work with him to build a *fantastic family!*

APPENDIX A
ASSESSING YOUR FAMILY'S STRENGTHS

The qualities of strong families can be broken down into six general categories, as outlined below. Put an "S," for *strength*, beside the qualities you feel your family has achieved, and a "G," for *growth*, beside those qualities that are areas of potential growth. If the particular characteristic does not apply to your family or is not a characteristic important to you, put an "NA," for *not applicable*.

By doing this exercise, family members will be able to identify those areas they would like to work on together to improve and those areas of strength that will serve as the foundation for their growth and positive change together.

THE ASSESSMENT TOOL

COMMITMENT

1._____ We are "always there" for each other.
2._____ We are dedicated to our marriage as the core of the family.
3._____ We (spouses) are faithful to each other sexually.
4._____ We value each family member as a precious part of the family.

5._____ We take care of each other and help each other.

6._____ We share many family goals.

7._____ We give family priority over outside activities, including work.

8._____ We are honest with each other.

9._____ We have numerous family traditions.

10._____ We will endure/stay together as a family.

11._____ We have unconditional love for each other.

12._____ We can depend on each other.

13._____ We make sacrifices for our family.

14._____ Give an overall rating (S or G) of *commitment* in your family.

APPRECIATION AND AFFECTION

15._____ We show appreciation to each other every day.

16._____ We feel deep and genuine affection for each other.

17._____ We avoid criticizing each other.

18._____ We speak positively to each other.

19._____ We recognize each other's accomplishments.

20._____ We see each other's good qualities.

21._____ We look for the good in each other (dig for diamonds).

22._____ We are sincere in expressions of appreciation.

23._____ We practice good manners at home and with others.

24._____ We refrain from sarcasm and put-downs.

25._____ We cultivate humor that is gentle and positive. (No one is embarassed or hurt by it.)

26._____ We accept compliments and kindnesses graciously.

27._____ We create a pleasant environment at home.

28._____ We enhance each other's self-esteem.

29._____ We feel safe and secure in our interactions with each other.

30._____ Give an overall rating (S or G) of *appreciation and affection* in your family

POSITIVE COMMUNICATION

31._____ We allow time for communication (conversations, discussions).

32._____ We have positive communication.

33._____ We listen to each other.

34._____ We check the meaning of messages (give feedback, seek clarification).

35._____ We see things from each other's point of view (have empathy).

36._____ We avoid criticizing, judging, or acting superior.

37._____ We are honest and truthful (and kind).

38._____ We deal with disagreements promptly.

39._____ We deal with conflict issues one at a time.

40._____ We are specific when dealing with conflict issues.

41._____ We seek compromise or consensus in resolving conflict (rather than "win or lose").

42._____ We avoid actions and words that would be emotionally devastating to each other.

43._____ We seek to understand and accept our differences.

44._____ Give an overall rating (S or G) of *positive communication* in your family.

TIME TOGETHER

45._____ We eat meals together regularly.

46._____ We do house and yard chores together.

47._____ We spend time together in recreation (play).

48._____ We participate in religious activities as a family.

49._____ We attend school or social activities together.

50._____ We celebrate holidays, birthdays, and anniversaries as a family.

51._____ We have a family vacation.

52._____ We enjoy each other's company.

53._____ We have good times together that are unplanned and spontaneous.

54._____ We take time to be with each other.

55._____ We spend good quality time together.

56._____ Give an overall rating (S or G) of *time together* in your family.

SPIRITUAL WELL-BEING

57._____ We believe that God has a purpose for our lives.

58._____ We have moral beliefs and values that guide us (honesty, responsibility).

59._____ We practice virtues such as patience, forgiveness, and controlling anger.

60._____ We have inner peace even in difficult times because of our relationship with God.

61._____ We have an outlook on life that is usually hopeful and confident.

62._____ We believe that God watches over and guides our family.

63._____ We are part of a church family.

64._____ We have family and friends who share our spiritual beliefs.

65._____ We praise God for his love for and involvement in our family.

66._____ We attend worship services as a family.

67._____ We read and study the Bible and other Christian literature.

68._____ We spend time each day in prayer.

69._____ We meditate on God's Word.

70._____ We apply our spiritual values to everyday life.

71._____ We avoid extreme or ongoing arguments over beliefs.

72._____ Give an overall rating (S or G) of *spiritual well-being* in your family.

ABILITY TO COPE WITH STRESS AND CRISES

73._____ We are able to ignore petty irritants and minor stresses.

74._____ We don't give lots of attention or energy to worry.

75._____ We believe that daily struggles/challenges are just a part of reaching a bigger goal.

76._____ We use humor to relieve stress and tension.

77._____ We take life one day at a time.

78._____ We eliminate some involvements when our schedules get too full.

79._____ We give attention/energy to the most important things first.

80._____ We engage in recreational activities and hobbies.

81._____ We enjoy outdoor relaxation and recreation.

82._____ We participate in regular exercise.

83._____ We manage to see some good in bad situations.

84._____ We work together to face the challenges of crises.

85._____ We support each other emotionally in crisis situations.

86._____ We seek help from friends, church, and neighbors during crises.

87._____ We seek professional help in crisis situations.

88._____ We call on spiritual resources (God's help, faith, hope) in times of crises.

89._____ We see opportunities for personal and family growth in crisis situations.

90._____ We use good communication to share feelings and to solve problems.

91._____ We are flexible and adaptable.

92._____ Give an overall rating (S or G) of *ability to cope with stress and crises* in your family.

APPENDIX B
RESOURCES TO HELP YOUR FAMILY BECOME FANTASTIC

Sometimes we all need a little help getting started on our do-it-yourself projects. Fortunately there are aids for families interested in becoming better.

BOOKS AND VIDEOS

In addition to this book, many other books and videos are available at bookstores and public libraries. Look for books about:

- communication
- managing finances
- parenting
- sexuality
- building self-esteem
- managing stress
- developing spirituality
- coping with divorce, death, unemployment, or illness

WEB SITES

There are a number of Web sites that contain good information about marriage and family relationships.

- ◆ Family Dynamics Institute's site lists specific tools you can use for your marriage and to increase your parenting skills. (www.familydynamics.net)

- ◆ Visit Marriage Builders' site for information, articles, a questions-and-answers section, and a subscription to a free newsletter. (www.marriagebuilders.com)

- ◆ The Cloverdale Center for Family Strengths (Dr. Donnie Hilliard, director) can be found through Faulkner University's site. (www.faulkner.edu)

- ◆ The Association for Couples in Marriage Enrichment sponsors marriage-enrichment seminars across the United States. (http://home.swbell.net/tgall/acme.htm)

- ◆ Information about marriage and family relationships, parenting, and other family-related issues may also be found at the Center for the Family. (www.pepperdine.edu/gsep/family)

Marriage-Enrichment Seminars

One of the most exciting developments in the field of family studies in the past twenty years has been the explosion of interest in prevention and enhancement. Marriage and family enrichment have grown by leaps and bounds as people have discovered the benefits of enhancing a basically sound marriage, rather than letting a relationship become terminally ill and then seeking a miracle cure.

Numerous marriage-enrichment programs can be found around the country. Look around, and you'll likely find one that suits your philosophy, values, and style, because there are several approaches to marital enrichment.

Some have a religious basis because they come out of churches; others do not because they are offered by community mental health centers, schools, or family service agencies. The format of marriage-enrichment programs varies as well. You'll find discussions, readings, lectures, videos, homework, and combinations of these techniques.

What else can you expect from marriage enrichment? Expect a pleasant association with other couples—some of them absolutely fascinating—interested in improving their marriages. Expect some fun and laughs and some work. Be prepared to discover that your problems aren't all that unique. Other couples will be having trouble with bossy in-laws, teens who are embarrassed to be seen with them, stubborn two-year-olds, balancing the checkbook, talking about sex, and more.

Expect your marriage—if it is basically sound—to improve, but don't expect drastic changes unless you allow God to work in you. Most enrichment programs last six to ten weeks, and that's usually not enough time to implement all the changes you'll learn to make. To increase their lasting effectiveness, many marriage-enrichment programs encourage couples to continue to meet on their own after the official meetings have concluded. Typically, couples meet for a potluck dinner and conversation on a monthly basis. Sometimes close friendships develop.

Family Dynamics Institute, of which Joe Beam is president, offers the following helpful courses:

♦ A special three-day seminar for those who need a jump-start because of problems such as an affair or other major difficulties

♦ An eight-week course for all marriages—those that are wonderful, those that are mediocre, and those that are troubled

The Cloverdale Center for Family Strengths at Faulkner University, of which Dr. Donnie Hilliard is director, offers a thirteen-week marriage-success curriculum for churches. *Marriage Success for You: Charting Your Marriage Destiny* is designed to be used as a Sunday or Wednesday class over the duration of a quarter.

FAMILY-ENRICHMENT SEMINARS

Just as there are wonderful courses and seminars for marriage, there are also wonderful courses and seminars for parenting and other family matters. Check you local organizations such as YWCAs and YMCAs for their offerings. Also, call churches in your area to discover how they can help.

Family Dynamics Institute offers these family-enrichment seminars:

- ◆ An eight-week parenting seminar designed by Dr. Nick Stinnett and written by Dr. Marilyn Stewart

- ◆ An eight-week course based on this book, designed to be taken by parents and children together

MARRIAGE AND FAMILY THERAPY

A marriage and family therapist can be great help for some situations. Some of you probably turned pale or blushed at that suggestion. The incorrect notion that only "crazy" people go to a counselor or therapist should really be turned around to say that some people are "crazy" *not* to go for help. Think about it: You aren't ashamed to haul your car to a mechanic when it makes strange noises; you call a plumber when the tub refuses to drain; and you call an electrician to handle a wiring problem. We don't expect to fill our own teeth, build our own homes, or fly our own airplanes. We depend on professionals.

Family relationship problems aren't really so different. If you haven't *learned* good communication skills or other relationship skills (just as people *learn* plumbing skills), you may benefit from outside help from a professional. A counselor also can be a neutral, objective helper in figuring out the dynamics in a family.

It's difficult to establish a rule of thumb concerning whether you need to visit a family therapist. Some symptoms that tend to indicate a need for a professional's help would include:

- ◆ spouse abuse, either physical or emotional
- ◆ child abuse or neglect
- ◆ alcohol or other drug abuse
- ◆ serious communication deficiencies
- ◆ prolonged depression
- ◆ a continuing extramarital affair
- ◆ repeated extramarital affairs
- ◆ children having considerable trouble at school or getting into trouble (vandalism, thefts, fights, gangs, drugs, alcohol)

◆ serious consideration of divorce

If you're in doubt, one or two visits with a therapist will help you decide if you want more.

How do you pick a good marriage and family therapist? Begin by looking at the person's professional qualifications. He or she should be willing to discuss background and training with you. Marriage and family counselors come from a number of different disciplines. Some are trained specifically for family counseling in a university or training center; others come from the more general professions of psychology, social work, family studies, psychiatry, or the ministry. Some counselors are certified by the American Association of Marriage and Family Therapists (AAMFT). This means they have done many hours of counseling under the supervision of experienced therapists.

You should ask prospective counselors about their approach or their philosophies of treatment. Some counselors use a family systems approach, others are behavioral therapists, and still others emphasize reality therapy or do nondirective counseling. Most use a combination of techniques. Each should be able to explain her or his approach in a way that you can understand. Be sure the approach makes sense to you personally.

Personal characteristics of counselors also vary widely. The best are usually kind, rational, honest, open, forgiving, humble, and humorous. You will be most comfortable with someone who has values similar to your own. It's a good idea to share your religious views and values at the outset and ask the counselor his or her values and beliefs. If his or her beliefs are dramatically different than yours, consider looking for another counselor.

If you know someone who has visited a therapist, ask for a recommendation. Like everything else, shop around.

You may wish to inquire about the counselor's fees. Generally these range from $50 to $125 or more per session. Some health insurance policies may pay a portion of counseling fees. Counselors and counseling agencies often charge on a sliding fee scale based on income. For example, one single parent went for help with the stress and loneliness of divorce. She was charged $5 per session based on her income.

Counseling need not go on indefinitely, but it may require several sessions to be successful. A minimum of six to eight sessions should be fair to both the counselor and the marriage. If significant progress can't be made in that time, other arrangements should be made. If good progress is being made, a family could stay with a counselor for a longer time depending upon the goals the family has set.

TRAINING TO HELP OTHERS

If you would like to help other families as well as your own, you might consider getting trained to teach some of the courses mentioned earlier.

Family Dynamics Institute conducts three-day training seminars every month across America and Canada to train laypeople how to help other families. You won't be a "counselor" at the end of those three days, but you will be equipped to facilitate the courses listed below through your church or organization. You can learn to teach the following courses that tremendously bless families:

- An eight-week interactive course for married couples
- An eight-week parenting course developed for Family Dynamics Institute by Dr. Nick Stinnett
- An eight-week interactive course for families based on this book

APPENDIX C

WHAT YOU, YOUR CHURCH, YOUR BUSINESS, AND YOUR COMMUNITY CAN DO FOR FAMILIES

The future of families in this country will be decided in great measure by what society does to enhance family potential. Individual families do not live in a vacuum. Many families want to develop their potential, but in a world of war, racism, sexism, ageism, unemployment, violence, and a host of societal and international problems, the task can be overwhelming. But if communities all work together, we can help more families than just our own. Families can be strengthened through a five-pronged approach that will impact most of the population in major areas of people's lives. The five-pronged approach begins at the individual level, then moves through churches, schools, corporations, and the media.

WHAT YOU CAN DO

This book has focused on what people can do to enhance their own family's development and what the family can do to improve itself. But by observing the people in strong families, it was also quite clear that their love for each other was often complemented by a love for people in other families in their community.

The strong family's commitment to a spiritual dimension of life—a life of principled service to God or humankind or some higher good—is reflected in their behavior toward people outside the family as well as inside the family.

One experienced, older mother of three (who knows exactly how frustrating children can be) said that whenever she goes shopping, she often sees a harried, younger mother with a wailing baby or a toddler running wild in the aisles. Anxious and embarrassed, the young mother may be about to pinch or spank the child.

The experienced mother has a kind way of helping. Casually and gently, she speaks to the mother, "I've got three kids. Whew! It's sure hard." And then she adds something, depending on circumstances, "Can he have this cracker?" or "I wish I had her energy." In this way, she calms the waters, saving a child from further pain and a frustrated parent from feelings of guilt and inadequacy.

With people we know from church, work, or the neighborhood, it's even easier to be supportive. We can sense when another person is upset, and rather than ignore her or him, we can become involved. This may mean simply listening and caring as they tell their tales of woe. It may mean a bit more.

"I feel so stupid," Ed told his neighbor. "I haven't had a job for five months. I just can't find one." Arlan had heard Ed yelling in frustration one morning and went next door to see what was wrong. Ed had been roaring with the full force his lungs could muster, and Arlan knew he needed help.

Arlan helped get the brakes and clutch fixed in Ed's car, and he called five friends to see if they knew of work. Ed doesn't have a job yet, but he doesn't feel totally alone in an uncaring world. "You kept me from running away from it all," he admitted sheepishly to Arlan. "I was about to leave Nancy and the kids. It would have really made things worse."

Other examples of the ways members of strong families reach out to other families include the following:

- ◆ coaching a soccer or baseball team for their own kids and a bunch of other people's kids

◆ taking the Girl Scout troop on a bicycle tour ("That was the greatest experience of my life," one girl told her leader, five years later.)

◆ helping a friend fix his roof, thus taking financial pressure off him

◆ taking food to the parents whose baby died and staying for several hours to talk and cry with them and eventually to eat the food with them

◆ offering to have some friends' teen stay over while they go on vacation for two weeks ("Oh, come on Dad! I'm sick of my sisters. Why can't I stay with Mr. and Mrs. Smith, huh?")

◆ serving as captain of the Neighborhood Watch crime-prevention program and taking time to chat with the older, isolated people on rounds to distribute literature

The list could be much longer. Wherever you serve families in ways that bring them joy and enhance their self-esteem, you support the development of stronger families. And in addition to the help you give to others, you will find that you are repaid tenfold in satisfaction and joy. Even people in crises find that they often are helped themselves by helping others. It gets their minds off troubles that might otherwise drown them. Even more important, serving others allows us to be the hands and feet of God in bringing goodness to our world.

WHAT CHURCHES CAN DO

If you are a leader in your church or if you exercise substantial influence there, you can help families in several ways. Even if you don't consider yourself a leader, you can help families if you are willing to take responsibility to teach a class or organize a support group or help plan a family-enrichment activity.

PREVENTION

A major part of the educational effort in most churches is aimed at the prevention of family problems. Serious family problems often start as small problems that could have been avoided or managed more effectively with a few easily learned skills. With prevention in mind, the topics for study are numerous: preparation for marriage, living as a single, financial management, balancing work and family, stress management, parenting, sexuality, alcohol and other drug abuse, retirement, dealing with conflict, building family strengths. And this list is not exhaustive.

These topics may be presented in a variety of formats. One possibility is to have discussion groups—with prepared leaders—that meet to discuss material they have already read. Workshops or seminars can be planned for a short block of time, such as a weekend; these can include a variety of activities such as guest speakers, films, small-group discussions, and brainstorming sessions. Of course, formal classes scheduled to meet regularly for several months are a mainstay of any educational effort. It may be helpful to arrange some classes of mixed age groups, such as teens and parents meeting together to learn about "Surviving Adolescence," for example.

People learn in different ways: Some learn best by seeing, some by hearing, some by doing. Although this is stated in simple terms, it does emphasize the need to offer ideas in a variety of forms. Teachers of classes and guest speakers may want to use audiovisuals, for example, to enhance their lectures. Group discussions expose learners to the valuable resource of other people's experiences. And talking about ideas seems to help most people incorporate them into everyday life. Posters, bulletin boards, newsletters, flyers, and pamphlets are other media for sharing information. If resources permit, a library of books, materials, and audio and videotapes is a bonus.

COUNSELING

Counseling is a natural part of a family-life education program, just as the services of a physician are part of a total healthcare effort. Consequently, many religious organizations provide counseling services for individuals and families under extreme stress or in a crisis situation.

A major thrust of counseling is education for more effective communication, problem solving, or decision making. Support groups of people with special needs often serve the joint purposes of teaching, counseling, and comforting. Possible support groups might include widows, single parents, grieving people, those with chronic illness, singles, divorced, those with addictive disorders, adoptive parents, or those caring for elderly family members.

ENRICHMENT

Families also need encouragement in the areas of their lives that are going well. Churches may offer marrage-enrichment seminars for couples, family-strengths seminars for the entire family, and also provide a variety of activities for families to participate in as a family, thus encouraging time together, shared interests, and family fun. These activities are oriented around recreation, service, learning, or worship and include the following: family camps or retreats, mother-daughter (father-daughter, mother-son, father-son) banquets, vacation Bible school, or all-church picnics. In other instances, high-school or college students and their parents are honored in a special ceremony at graduation; teens plan, cook, and serve a meal to "appreciate" their parents; parent-child teams fill boxes with food for those in need; or volunteers help the infirm people with household chores or shopping.

OUTREACH

Finally, most churches aim to serve non-Christian members of their community. Churches sometimes offer seminars, lectures, or workshops on family topics to the public. These are free or inexpensive and may have childcare or refreshments as an added incentive to attend. Other services that might be offered to the community include meals to shut-ins; tutoring; job placement; food pantry; preschool, mom's day out or daycare; daycare of adults; counseling services for divorce, addictive behaviors, or family violence.[1]

WHAT CORPORATIONS CAN DO

If you are an executive with decision-making authority, a board member, or have substantial influence in the decisions of your company, you can serve families in several ways.

FAMILY-FRIENDLY POLICIES

Because most people have jobs, reaching families through the workplace is a logical and strategic avenue for strengthening families. The development of family-friendly personnel policies has great potential to benefit families. One such practice is flextime, which allows employees flexibility in setting the hours they work. For example, workers choose to come to work at 6, 7, 8, or 9 A.M.; lunch is a variable length; quitting time depends on the time of starting and the length of lunch. This allows workers to get children off to school or to be home to greet them or to accommodate a spouse's work schedule. Some companies have developed a policy that allows employees to do portions of their work at home, such as transcribing records, typing, or bookkeeping.

Other family-oriented personnel policies include shared and part-time jobs and supportive leave policies. For example, few companies in America currently offer paternity leave. Yet this practice is common in many other countries, and paternity leave can certainly be an important help to families. Imagine having Dad at home to tend his new baby while Mom gets a nap. Longer maternity leaves would also benefit families. Citizens of several other countries around the world are shocked to learn that the standard practice in the U.S. is to offer six weeks of maternity leave. For some countries, such as Norway, the standard length of maternity leave is six *months*.

Childcare services on the workplace premises can be a tremendous support as families integrate family life with the work world and seek to reduce stress and anxiety. A parent can have lunch with a child or check on a child during the day (at breaktime), and the child feels safe knowing the parent is nearby.

A recent news story featured the family-friendly work environment of a large corporation. Employees have many benefits including on-site childcare, an excercise gym (and classes), a medical clinic, fine art throughout the building, live piano concerts at mealtimes, landscaped grounds that encourage a relaxing walk, and a policy that no one may stay after 6 P.M. to work. These benefits cost millions to provide but save the company millions more in decreased employee turnover and increased productivity.

FAMILY-LIFE EDUCATION PROGRAMS

Family-life education programs could be offered regularly through the employer on topics such as parenting, communication, financial management, caring for elderly parents, stress management, or marriage enrichment. Such experiences benefit not only families but the employer as well. There is a strong link between a strong, stable, happy family life and higher levels of productivity and morale and lower rates of absenteeism. When workers are happy and not worried about what is going on at home, they can be more focused and successful in their work.

POSITIVE WORKPLACE ENVIRONMENT

When leaders of corporations create a positive environment in the workplace, not only are the lives of the employees enriched, but the general health and morale of the organization is improved. Leaders can apply the qualities of strong families—such as good communication patterns, the expression of appreciation, and commitment—to the relationships within the organization so that there is a feeling of family-like closeness and commitment at work.

BUSINESS-TO-BUSINESS RELATIONSHIPS

The qualities of strong families can even be applied in business relationships. Kimball Bullington, as the materials manager at Micro Motion, Inc., a subsidiary of Emerson Electric Company, was responsible for the timely delivery of quality materials at competitive prices.

He was also responsible for maintaining good relationships with approximately five hundred suppliers of materials.

In the spring of 1995, Micro Motion, Inc., began using a slightly modified version of the six qualities of strong families in their relationships with suppliers. The industries Kimball related to included foundries, electronic cable manufacturers, forge shops, tubing mills, aluminum die casters, instrumentation manufacturers, machine shops, and suppliers of paper products.

"The response to our new methods was overwhelmingly positive," noted Kimball. "At the same time, performance indicators rose. We believe the emphasis on effective *communication* and the frequent and appropriate expression of *appreciation* to our suppliers enhanced communication and built commitment."[2]

WHAT SCHOOLS CAN DO

If you serve on a school board, hold an executive position in a school system, are a teacher, or are active in PTA/PTO, you can have substantial influence on the decisions of a school and can help the families in your community.

FAMILY-LIFE CURRICULUM

A powerful way to strengthen families through the schools is for each state to establish a comprehensive family-life curriculum in kindergarten through grade twelve. Human-relationship skills are learned (just as math or geography). Children can learn how to communicate effectively and kindly, to settle conflicts without violence, to nurture others, to solve problems, and to care about others.

FAMILY PROGRAMS

Schools may empower families by arranging programs that promote the health and well-being of all family members. Seminars, workshops, and resource materials can be offered on topics such as parent education, family enrichment, stress management, alcohol and other drug abuse, nutrition, physical fitness, reducing violence in the community, and gangs. Resource materials could be provided for parents who choose not to attend seminars. Videotaped seminars or workshops can be made available to parents who cannot attend or who have difficulty reading printed materials.

FAMILY RESOURCE CENTER

Some schools, such as Salome Urena Middle Academics in New York, have a family resource center that is staffed by parents and other volunteers and is open from 8:30 A.M. to 8:30 P.M. Such centers provide education and services in a variety of areas—from teaching parenting skills to helping parents complete their own high-school equivalency degrees.

PARENTAL INVOLVEMENT

Parental involvement in the daily activities at the school can be increased by use of parent volunteers to assist with enrollment and registration, office chores, library, sick room, preparation of classroom materials, and ticket and concession sales at athletic events. Also, plans can be implemented for bringing students, parents, and teachers together for family-oriented assemblies, class breakfasts, and ice-cream socials.

FAMILY-FRIENDLY ENVIRONMENT

Schools can develop an environment of *school as family*. A more family-friendly school can be structured for students, parents, and employees. Entire multigrade curricula on the family can be developed. The whole school, as well as each class, can come to resemble a family by establishing the characteristics of a strong family, such as effective communication and commitment to a group identity.

A SCHOOL SUCCESS STORY

The Florida State University School—which educates kindergarten through grade twelve—is a demonstration school for The Family/School/Community Partnership Program. Virginia Bert and Kathleen Funderburk—two pioneers in the concept of family/school/community partnerships—built this program on the premise that the school is in a unique position to reach and involve most families in a partnership effort. After all, most communities have a school, and many people in the community will have children or grandchildren in school.

Efforts were made to create an atmosphere of family closeness among the faculty, staff, and students in the demonstration school. Parents are encouraged to become involved at the school and to participate in numerous educational activities. The school's central plaza area has picnic tables where students, faculty, and parents can eat lunch or relax in the fresh air. Parents collect tickets at basketball games; and students, siblings, and parents interact together in the gym.

The six characteristics of strong families formed the foundation of the program model and were used in the family-education programs, the school curriculum, and in guiding the supportive partnerships among the families, the school, and the community.

The Family/School/Community Partnership Program has received community support and cooperation from businesses, churches, social service agencies, and the local media. Students, parents, and teachers support the community by such practices as visiting nursing homes.

The results of this partnership have been very successful. Communication, support, and mutual involvement among the families, school, and the community were significantly enhanced. Florida education commissioner Betty Castor remarked, "I think it is safe to say that they have done more than any single school to perfect family involvement."[3]

When a program such as the Family/School/Community Partnership program succeeds, society benefits in several ways: Families are improved, strengthened, empowered. Children are more successful in school and experience a greater degree of personal well-being. Communities become more supportive, caring, pleasant places in which to live. Social problems decline.

WHAT THE COMMUNITY CAN DO

If you are a leader in your community, have substantial influence there, or are willing to get involved, you can help create caring environments to nurture the families who live there. Caring environments must be created; they do not "just happen."

THE WILLARD COMMUNITY FAMILY-STRENGTHS PROGRAM

An excellent example of families and elements of the community working together can be found in Lincoln, Nebraska, where an exciting community endeavor—the Willard Community Family Strengths Program—was developed in response to a pressing community need. This particular neighborhood—the old Willard School District—had disturbingly high rates of vandalism and juvenile delinquency. It was the imaginative idea of Lela Watts, the director of the Willard Community Center at the time, to meet the delinquency problem with a total family approach.

A program was begun through the Willard Community Center to build the strengths and skills of the families and youth in the neighborhood. Building self-esteem, communication skills, and expanding the scope of activities that entire families could enjoy were the areas of focus for the Willard Family Strengths Program.

One consequence of the program was that a spirit of teamwork emerged among the families in the community. They took the initiative and worked together to make long-overdue repairs on buildings and sidewalks. They made improvements to the community center building and experienced an improved community pride and identity.

The most dramatic result of the Willard Family Strengths Program was that the delinquency and vandalism rates were reduced by 83 percent within a six-month period. Two years after the program was started, delinquency and vandalism rates were reduced virtually to zero.

The Willard Family Strengths Program was not expensive or hard to implement, yet the results were astonishing. This kind of program might not be enough for a seriously crime-ridden, inner-city neighborhood. However, most neighborhoods are not crime-ridden, inner-city war zones. And they could be improved by programs such as this—without a lot of red tape, cost, or difficulty.

NASHVILLE COOPERATION

Another creative model of how a community can create a positive, supportive environment for families can be found in Nashville, Tennessee. Tennessee State University, one of Nashville's institutions of higher learning; the *Nashville Banner*, one of Tennessee's major newspapers; and the Kroger grocery store chain cooperated on this community effort, which included Nashville and most of Middle Tennessee.

Tennessee State University researchers Patricia Wyatt and Barbara Nye conducted a survey designed to help families in Middle Tennessee to look at their own strengths and to become even stronger. The *Nashville Banner* carried a series of articles on the study, which were written by staff writer Lady Hereford. The *Nashville Banner* included a copy of the Family-Strengths Inventory in the paper and invited readers to participate. Support from the business community was provided by the Kroger company, which gave a gift certificate worth five hundred dollars in free groceries. Families who participated in the study were included in the drawing for the five-hundred-dollar gift certificate.

This project sent a message from three major components of the community—a newspaper, a university, and a retailer—that families are important. The high visibility of this cooperative project helped establish the idea that families are valued and are a top priority. This project also helped families become more aware of their strengths and encouraged family members to focus more on each other's good qualities.

WHAT THE MEDIA CAN DO

If your children watch TV, play with computers, or involve themselves with media in any form, this section is for you. If you are a station manager, network executive, newspaper or magazine editor, soft-ware developer, or have any other position of influence in the realm of media, you can affect families in your community and beyond.

Never underestimate the power of the media to influence the quality of family life. On the average, families have the television turned on more than seven hours a day. By the time children reach the age of eighteen, they will have spent more hours in front of the television than in the classroom. That television affects behavior is clear. Decades of research have shown that passive consumption of commercial television can lead to attention deficit, nonreflective thinking, and confusion between reality and packaged representations.[4]

It probably comes as no surprise to you that the food products that children and adolescents consume while watching television are the same as those advertised on TV. They are primarily high in fat, sugar, or sodium.[5] Ironically, there are also many messages that everyone, but especially girls and women, must be thin and attractive to be accepted. It is no stretch of the imagination that such media messages contribute to the development of eating disorders such as anorexia and bulimia.

Considerable evidence exists that viewing a great deal of violence can increase aggressive feelings and behavior.[6] Consider also the fact that so many of the situation comedies on television are dominated by hostile humor characterized by put-downs, sarcasm, ridicule, and insults. It's reasonable to assume that adults and children who watch several hours of this programming may begin to believe (perhaps unconsciously) that hostile humor is a desirable or funny way to relate to others. If they imitate this behavior, their relationships will likely suffer. No one wants to be made to appear foolish!

Incidents of irresponsible sex, violence, and anti-family messages have dramatically increased during the last forty years. The images of family life portrayed in the media leave much to be desired.

PUBLIC DEMANDS FOR CHANGE

What can be done besides turning off the television? One powerful option that has not been pursued in earnest is a loud public clamor for change. If families, schools, churches, businesses, and community organizations joined forces in asking for (demanding) changes in the content of movies and television, changes would come surprisingly fast.

MEDIA SELF-REGULATION

The media can do much in the realm of self-regulation. The American media industries have adopted certain self-regulatory strategies that help. For example, film and television entertainment executives have taken action in recent years to avoid glamorizing alcohol, tobacco, and other drugs. However, there are still inconsistencies in the efforts.

RATING SYSTEMS

The cable television networks and the video game industry have developed rating systems and advisories to help parents monitor what their children view and play. Yet much stronger regulations are needed to foster more positive programming for families. It is interesting that every other Western nation has stronger regulations than the U.S. regarding educational programming for children.[7]

MEDIA LITERACY

Parents can help their children and every member of the family become *media literate*, that is, develop the skills to analyze and evaluate media messages critically. For example, parents can watch television programs and video games and listen to some popular songs with their children. Family discussions can then explore the nature of the messages and the implications of those messages. Adults may wish to encourage the inclusion of media-literacy skills in school curricula and community programs. Although such efforts are in the infant stages in the U.S., media-literacy is a required component of the language arts curriculum for grades seven through twelve in Australia, Canada, Great Britain, and Spain.[8]

POWERFUL POTENTIAL

Despite instances of negative influence by the media on families, there is great potential for the media to be used as a powerful tool to strengthen families. Videocassettes, music videos, video games, movies, computers, and television offer opportunities for entertainment and education. Computers, for example, are a growing influence in homes. Why not develop interactive family-life education programs to inform about finances, parenting, communication, dealing with difficult people, nutrition, or a number of other topics? Media can provide images of family that are positive and that promote compassion, critical thinking, and values.

MEDIA CAMPAIGNS

We can do much to create a more supportive environment for families by launching media campaigns to increase the visibility of healthy families and to communicate the message that families are important and valued. For example, public service messages can be designed for use in radio, television, and newspapers to encourage behavior that will promote healthy relationships and stronger families. Families, healthcare organizations, businesses, schools, churches, and other community organizations can work cooperatively with the media to develop such messages.

Another example of how a media campaign might work is the act of proclaiming a "day of the family," "week of the family," or "month of the family." Recently, the United Nations designated May 15 as the International Day of the Family. This simple but powerful symbol communicates to mothers, fathers, and children that what they do in their families and for their families is important and is valued by someone else.

APPENDIX D

MORE ABOUT THE
FAMILY-STRENGTHS RESEARCH

A nthropologist Margaret Mead believed that the family is the most difficult institution in any human society to study because it is a relatively closed system, troublesome for outsiders to penetrate and understand. Each family-strengths study conducted with families across the country and around the world presented innumerable challenges: finding the right research team for the study at hand; deciding whether to use quantitative research methods focusing on numbers and statistics or qualitative methods focusing on explaining processes and family dynamics; securing funding; crossing language barriers, cultural variations, and political boundaries. Each study, thus, was a distinctly unique challenge, and the approaches utilized in every instance differed dramatically.

INITIAL ASSUMPTIONS

Dr. Nick Stinnett began the research on strong families by making some basic assumptions of what strong families would be like. Using his knowledge about family relations as a guide, Dr. Stinnett made three assumptions about strong families: (1) members would have a high degree of marital happiness; (2) they would have satisfying parent-child relationships; and (3) they would do a good job of meeting each other's needs.

Developing the Family-Strengths Inventory

The instrument for the initial family-strengths research over twenty-five years ago was a questionnaire having both open-ended and fixed-alternative type questions. The questions included were based upon a review of what the professional literature suggested might be related to family success or strength. Before the questions were submitted to families, they were given to a panel of judges (family-life experts holding a doctoral or master's degree in human development and family studies). The judges were asked to evaluate each of the questions in the questionnaire in the following ways: Is the question relevant to the topic being investigated? Is the question clear? Do other questions need to be added? After the panel of judges responded to the questionnaire, a pretest was administered to a small number of families.

The final form of the questionnaire (referred to as the Family-Strengths Inventory) was then administered to a sample of 130 strong families in Oklahoma. Analysis of that data indicated that the six qualities that the strong families had in common were: a high degree of commitment, expressed appreciation, good communication patterns, much time spent together, a high degree of religious orientation, and the ability to deal with stress and crises in a positive manner.

Later, this sample of strong families was compared to a sample of families that had experienced divorce within the previous six months. These families were questioned, using the same questionnaire, about their relationship prior to the divorce. A sample of families experiencing severe relationship problems who were receiving counseling at state agencies was also compared to the group of strong families. The divorced families and the families with serious relationship problems expressed to a highly significant degree far less of the six qualities than did the strong families. In many cases, the divorced families and the families with the relationship problems were completely lacking in all of the six qualities.

The Family-Strengths Inventory was shortened before use in the national and international studies that followed. Statistical analysis of the revised Family-Strengths Inventory has shown that each of the items (reflecting the six qualities) was highly discriminating between those families with a high degree of family strength and those families with lower degrees of family strength. The questionnaire has been tested in many different studies with remarkably similar results.

THE FIRST STUDY

In his initial work at Oklahoma State University, Dr. Stinnett and a team of graduate-student researchers contacted Cooperative Extension Agents in each of Oklahoma's counties and asked them to recommend a few families that seemed to fit the assumptions about strong families. The Extension Agents were chosen because of their background training in family life, their concern for improving the quality of life for families, and their extensive personal contact with families in the community.

In order to simplify the analysis of the information collected, Dr. Stinnett also asked that the marriage be the first for both husband and wife, that both spouses be present (so that the marital relationship could be examined), and that the family have at least one child living at home (so that the parent-child relationship could be examined).[1]

Questionnaires were mailed to the families recommended by the specialists. Included in the questionnaire were questions asking the participants to rate their satisfaction with their marriage and their satisfaction with their relationships with their child or children. People who reported a high degree of marriage happiness and good parent-child relationships were included in the study. A few people were eliminated because their rating of either marital or parent-child relationships was not positive. The intent was to study strong families. That only a few families were eliminated indicates the accuracy of the Extension Agents in their recommendations.

A total of 130 families contributed information about their family life. The families were diverse in terms of socioeconomic status, race, ethnic origin, religion, and education. They came from rural and urban areas.

The questionnaire (the Family-Strengths Inventory) used in the study was long and garnered vast amounts of raw data. In fact, there was too much information to deal with in one huge chunk, so some data were stored for later use. Then as time and interest allowed, data were retrieved. For example, David Tomlinson, a graduate student at Oklahoma State University, was interested in the power structure in strong families. He went to the stored data to see how strong family members answered questions dealing with power structure (Who makes major decisions in the family? How are those are made?). Other graduate students conducted similar investigations; some sent another questionnaire or conducted interviews with the families to gather additional information.

Using information from the Family-Strengths Inventory, follow-up questionnaires, and interviews, Dr. Stinnett and his graduate-student teams looked at demographic characteristics of strong families, communication patterns, how they spent their time, marital satisfaction, life philosophies, personality characteristics, power structure, parent-child relationships, family commitment, relationship patterns, how they handled conflict, how they coped with crises, and religious orientation.

THE STUDY EXPANDS

In 1977, the Stinnetts moved to Lincoln, Nebraska, and the research was expanded nationwide. John DeFrain and graduate students Greg Sanders and Karen Strand joined the research group, and a slight change in procedure was made. Instead of having families recommended, volunteers were sought. Different methods were utilized for securing samples in the studies that followed.

In some of these studies, the sample was obtained by running a news story in newspapers throughout the nation and asking for volunteers to participate. These samples of strong families included those who responded to the news story and who also rated themselves very high on marriage happiness and satisfaction with the parent-child relationship. Newspapers in all sections of the United States were asked to cooperate by running this small news story:

STRONG FAMILIES NEEDED FOR NATIONAL RESEARCH

Lincoln, NE—Researchers at the University of Nebraska are seeking volunteers for a nationwide study of strong families.

"If you live in a strong family, we'd like you to contact us by mail," Dr. Nick Stinnett, chairperson of the Department of Human Development and the Family noted. "We know a lot these days about what makes families fail, but we really need to know a lot more about what makes families succeed. Your help is urgently requested."

Four dozen newspapers in twenty-five states printed the news story. A few days later, letters from volunteers started to pour in. Dozens of letters came each day for several weeks as people from several hundred families responded to the appeal. When the tiny story appeared in *The Minneapolis Star,* sixty-seven letters were received from strong families in the Twin Cities area alone. A Vermont paper called for information to write a larger story on the study, and responses from New England arrived. Papers in Iowa, South Carolina, and Oregon did likewise.

The response was overwhelming. American families were not going down the tubes; they were simply waiting for someone to ask the question, "What is right with families?" Many people wrote letters thanking the team for doing research on the positive aspects of family life.

Those who responded were sent the Family-Strengths Inventory, which had more than a hundred questions on how their family functioned. The questions covered many aspects of family life. No payment was given to volunteers aside from the team's gratitude and a short summary of the results of the project. The major benefit the volunteers derived was the satisfaction of contributing to the largest body of knowledge the scientific community has assembled on strong families. Once again, enormous amounts of raw data were gathered from the completed questionnaires. As in the work in Oklahoma, follow-up questionnaires were sent to some families and interviews were conducted with others.

After the first national study of strong families, several more national studies and a number of international studies were completed using a different sample of families with each study. In some studies, the strong families were obtained by running a news story—as in the first national study. For others, families were selected randomly for the purpose of comparing high-strength and low-strength families. Research has also been completed comparing recently divorced families with families exhibiting a high degree of strength.

OTHER RESEARCHERS JOINED THE STUDY

Graduate-student and faculty researchers have participated in the efforts to explore various facets of strength in families. For example, Dr. Jerry King, currently a professor of sociology at Arkansas State University, found tremendous similarities between blacks and whites when he made an intensive study of African-American family strengths. Julie Elmen and Judy Fricke made a national study of single parents (both male and female), focusing on family strengths and how they developed. Robin Smith and David Tucker examined strengths and stresses of executive families.

Dr. Pat Knaub and Sharon Hanna joined with Dr. Stinnett to study the strengths of remarried families. David Lynn explored the relationship between family strengths and personal well-being. Barbara Knorr focused on how good families cope with crises. Geraldine Gutz, Steve Johnson, Dr. Barbara Chesser, and Mel Luetchens investigated how family-strengths concepts could be used successfully in marriage-enrichment and family-life programs. Timothy Rampey studied the relationships among family strengths, religiosity, and purpose in life. Dr. Doug Abbott and Dr. Bill Meredith compared the strengths of European-American, African-American, Latino-American, Native-American, and Asian-American families and found the five groups to be remarkably similar, arguing that "the traits of strong families extend beyond ethnic boundaries."

Jon Wuerffel was interested in how humor related to the other family strengths and found that strong families tend to be fun families. (Football fans will remember the University of Florida's stellar quarter-back, Danny Wuerffel—Jon's son.) Dr. Pat Knaub looked at the strengths of dual-career families through the eyes of the mothers and the children. Dr. Stinnett conducted a large-scale study of the strengths of families with well-adjusted and happy adolescents. Susan Dahl and Dr. John DeFrain studied the strengths of families with a member who has a developmental disability. Nikki DeFrain, Linda Ernst, and Dr. John DeFrain examined how some people who suffer through a traumatic childhood can grow up to be healthy, happy adults with successful families.

INTERNATIONAL STUDIES

When some of the research turned to families outside the United States, the logical question was: "Would good families in other parts of the world be like the U.S. families?" Cultural differences could exist that might make interesting variations. As a result, the research was expanded in collaboration with Constanza Casas to include Central and South American families. Verna Weber completed a study of strengths of black families in South Africa. Bettina Stoll, a graduate student from Stuttgart, investigated family strengths in a sample of families from Germany, Austria, and Switzerland.

Russell Porter, pre-*glasnost*, wanted to study the strengths of Russian families but had to settle for a study of Russian families who had recently emigrated to the U.S. Yuh-hsien Chen examined the strengths of Taiwanese and Chinese families who had recently emigrated to the U.S. Dr. Kelley Brigman and Dr. Stinnett were interested in the strengths of Iraqi families and studied them a few years before the Gulf War broke out. Dr. John DeFrain backpacked into remote Tarahumara Indian villages in Chihuahua, Mexico, to learn more about the families living there; Nikki DeFrain reviewed the anthropological literature on these families, gleaning more about their strengths. Xiaolin Xie, Dr. John DeFrain, and Dr. Bill Meredith combined to work on a study of family strengths in urban and rural China. Dr. Stinnett and Anotai Jittrapanun studied family strengths in Thailand: Stinnett and Gum-Soon Chae did the same in South Korea. Dr. Nilufer Medora, Dr. Geoff Leigh, and Dr. John DeFrain are working on a study of strong families in India, while Dr. Doug Abbott prepares for his own Fulbright-sponsored study of strengths and challenges in poor families in India. Kathleen Wild hopes to study families in Brazil.

John and Nikki DeFrain and their daughters, Alyssa, Erica, and Amie, along with Jennifer Lepard, learned about family strengths in the South Pacific during a seven-month stay in Fiji. Their work there was supported by a Fulbright Scholarship, a faculty development scholarship from the University of Nebraska, and the University of the South Pacific in Suva, Fiji. The family plans to return to the islands soon to continue the work.

SLIGHTLY DIFFERENT METHODS IN OTHER CULTURES

To conduct research on family strength in other cultures and countries around the world is much more difficult than conducting research in the U.S., but it is wonderfully rewarding. At times it is possible to use questionnaire techniques for the studies, such as the team did in Austria, West Germany, Switzerland, Latin America, South Korea, Thailand, and China. The Family-Strengths Inventory obviously must be translated into the appropriate language and carefully checked to see if it is sensitive to the unique aspects of the particular culture being studied. Often the best questions asked were the open-ended questions: What are the strengths of your family? What makes your family work well? Why is your family so successful and happy? People answered in their own words and often told detailed and touching stories of their families.

In some cultures it was useful to include checklists of various family strengths so that comparisons could be made from culture to culture. This is difficult to do with absolute precision, for cultures use language and look at the world in different ways. In China, for example, the general family-strengths model used in the U.S. research described the strengths of Chinese families quite adequately. But as is true in every other culture, there are unique ways of experiencing the world in China.

The Chinese view positive communication, time together, and the ability to cope with stress and crises as primary family strengths, as strong families do in the U.S. The sample of families in China also emphasized formal education as a key to the success of the family. In traditional Chinese fashion, respect for elders (filial piety) and ethics education (training of the young in traditional Chinese values) are especially important.

Even when these strengths are present in a family, however, the Chinese still would not be prone to say that love existed in the family, for *love* is a word that does not resonate as well in China as it does in the U.S. Instead, the Chinese would be likely to say that the demonstration of the various family strengths indicates there is *harmony* in the family. As you can see, the basic dynamics are quite similar to U.S. culture, though the details and the terms the Chinese use may differ to some degree. The Chinese studies were conducted using questionnaire techniques and some interviews and observations of families in action.

In contrast, in the study of family strengths in the South Pacific, the DeFrain family quickly found that questionnaire techniques would not work well in Fiji, a culture with a long tradition of oral communication. Fijians love to talk and were always helpful when asked about how their families functioned. But few were very excited about filling out a questionnaire. (Who would blame them? A pleasant chat is always more fun!)

The Fijians taught clearly that family bonds are more important than money: Pacific islanders have created a way of life that emphasizes "sharing and caring" over the competitive individualism that permeates the social fabric of the U.S. today. We could all benefit from this great lesson taught by villagers in the South Pacific.

When Verna Weber went to South Africa, she discovered that immersing herself in African culture was the best approach to learning about healthy families. Verna went almost every day for a two-year period into Soweto, a black community outside Johannesburg. She came to know eleven families who were functioning well in a very hostile environment. The time was 1982–1984, and black families were living under apartheid, the centuries-old system of segregation and oppression by the white South African government.

Soweto was a poor, crowded, often violent, and demoralized community. The families often faced unemployment, hunger, health problems, chemical dependency, and racism. And yet, in spite of the difficulties of the decaying township in which they lived, these eleven families that Verna focused on managed to construct a reasonably positive emotional environment for their members. Verna saw their accomplishments as wonderful examples of the amazing power of the family spirit to transcend despair.

The description of life in Soweto, as Verna saw it, accurately describes life in any inner city in the U.S.—hunger, violence, chemical dependency, unemployment, and racism. Here, too, are reminders that the power of good families will overcome adverse conditions.

UNDERLYING SIMILARITIES AMONG CULTURES

Most of the fourteen thousand families contributing to this research have been from the United States, with about 10 percent from other countries around the world. Families in twelve countries in Central and South America, South Africa, Iraq, Thailand, South Korea, China, Taiwan, Fiji, Germany, Austria, Switzerland, India, Canada, and Mexico have participated.

One key to the successful study of family strengths in other coutries has been adaptability. Rather than trying to fit a culture into the U.S. model of family strengths, the researchers adapted their methods to fit the culture they were studying.

Another key to the successful study of strengths in families around the world has been taking a balanced approach. The researchers have looked at both differences and similarities in cultures and families. At first glance, some of the environments, cultures, and families appeared to be very different and unfamiliar. However, as the research progressed, it became clear that the dynamics of family behavior were very familiar. Families around the world are remarkably alike.

In spite of cultural differences, this research has shown that good families around the world share more similarities than differences. Others who have done multicultural research on key elements of the human condition bolster this postition. People are people are people. Families are families are families.

THE STUDY CONTINUES

Many questions wait to be answered; so as research budgets, time, and energies allow, other dimensions of family strengths are explored. A new sample of families is selected; questionnaires, interviews, and/or observation schedules are developed; and another set of data is collected. Because one size does not fit all, new approaches are created for each culture studied. Methods of investigation are developed that are sensitive to the particular culture being studied. This takes considerable time and effort, but the results are inspiring.

Dr. Stinnett, Dr. Donnie Hilliard, and Dennis Boytim are currently collecting data on strong families in Russia and the Ukraine. The DeFrains are studying and lecturing about family strengths in Australia. And so the Family-Strengths Research Project continues in the U.S. and around the world. It's simply too interesting and too much fun to stop. There is much more to learn about strong families in our own country, and the surface has only been scratched in regard to research in other cultures.

◆ NOTES ◆

PREFACE. SOME THINGS YOU NEED TO KNOW

1. To find out more about this powerful, fun, and effective inter-active course and how it can bless your family, call Family Dynamics Institute at 1-800-650-9995. FDI also offers other courses and resources on such family-related topics as marriage enrichment and parenting.

INTRODUCTION. WHAT MAKES A FAMILY STRONG, HEALTHY, AND HAPPY?

1. 1 Timothy 5:8.
2. Esther 4:14.
3. Esther 8:6.
4. The findings of other family researchers support the findings presented in this book. Dr. Herbert Otto, who was at the University of Utah in Salt Lake City in the early 1960s, is regarded as a pioneer in the area of healthy family functioning. He and his colleague, J. Gabler, surveyed the professional literature between 1947 and 1962, focusing on writings in sociology, psychology, anthropology, psychiatry, family-life education, and related fields. They found that researchers talked about 515 different qualities or traits possessed by successful families.

(The Family-Strengths Inventory titled "Assessing Your Family's Strengths" has more than fifty subcategories to illustrate the six main qualities.)

Dr. David Olson, from the University of Minnesota, Saint Paul, narrowed these down to three major qualities of strong families (D. H. Olson, & J. DeFrain, *Marriage and the Family: Systems, Diversity, and Strengths* [Mountain View, Calif.: Mayfield, 1996]). His research and this research complement each other perfectly.

Other prominent scholars across the country have models of "normal" families or "healthy" families with eight or twelve or fifteen qualities included. These models and this research are also in agreement. The issue is not how many qualities it takes to define a strong family. The important thing to keep in mind is that there is remarkable agreement among researchers and scholars regarding the general outline of what constitutes a strong family. If you'd like to read more about the other research mentioned here, see M. Krysan, K. A. Moore, & N. Zill, *Identifying Successful Families: An Overview of Constructs and Selected Measures* (Washington, D.C.: Child Trends, 1990).

CHAPTER 1. STEP ONE ◆ COMMIT TO YOUR FAMILY

1. K. W. Simon, "Fatherhood in the Middle Years" (master's thesis, University of Nebraska, Lincoln, 1982).

2. Malachi 2:13–16.

3. Matthew 19:8.

4. Ephesians 5:25.

5. Ephesians 5:28.

6. Ephesians 5:28.

7. Titus 2:4.

8. For more information on specialized interactive courses that guide husbands and wives to the deepest levels of love and intimacy, contact Family Dynamics Institute, the nonprofit organization led by Joe Beam, at 1-800-650-9995.

9. The following books are quite interesting: W. H. Masters, V. Johnson, & R. C. Kolodny, *Masters & Johnson on Sex and Human*

Loving (Boston: Little, Brown, 1986); and idem, *Human Sexuality*, 4th ed. (New York: Harper Collins, 1992).

10. Leviticus 20:10.

11. Hebrews 13:4.

12. For more information about how affairs happen, the various types of affairs, and how to find healing; see Joe Beam, *Becoming One* (West Monroe, La.: Howard Publishing, 1999).

13. See also Drs. Harley and Chalmers, *Surviving an Affair* (Old Tappan, N.J.: Fleming Revell Company, 1998).

14. 1 Timothy 5:16.

15. 1 Timothy 5:8.

16. Matthew 16:26.

17. Ephesians 4:25.

18. See Exodus 13 and Deuteronomy 6 for the basis for the tradition.

19. Mark 12:30.

20. Ephesians 5:25, 28; Colossians 3:19.

21. Galatians 5:14.

CHAPTER 2. STEP TWO ◆ EXPRESS APPRECIATION AND AFFECTION

1. Luke 17:15–19.

2. Matthew 22:37.

3. 1 Corinthians 7:3–5.

4. Leviticus 19:18; Matthew 19:19; 22:39; Mark 12:31, 33; Luke 10:27; Romans 13:9; Galatians 5:14; James 2:8.

5. This quote comes from Pablo Casals, *Joys and Sorrows: Reflections by Pablo Casals As Told to Albert E. Kahn* (New York: Simon and Schuster, 1970), 295.

CHAPTER 3. STEP THREE ◆ SHARE POSITIVE COMMUNICATION

1. Ephesians 4:31. See the urging for "speaking" the truth in love in the passages that precede.

2. Proverbs 15:22.

3. 1 Kings 19:4.

4. 1 Kings 19:10.

5. 1 Kings 19:18.

6. Job 42:4.

7. Ephesians 4:29.

8. Ephesians 4:25.

9. Ephesians 4:15.

10. Mark 10:42–45.

11. Ephesians 4:26.

CHAPTER 4. STEP FOUR ◆ SPEND TIME TOGETHER

1. Carnegie Council on Adolescent Development, *Great Transitions: Preparing Adolescents for a New Century* (New York: Carnegie Corporation of New York, 1995).

2. Ecclesiastes 3:1–8.

3. Ecclesiastes 2:24.

4. Ecclesiastes 4:9–12.

5. Ecclesiastes 5:12.

6. Ecclesiastes 6:3.

7. 1 Timothy 6:10.

8. Ephesians 5:15–16.

CHAPTER 5. STEP FIVE ◆ NURTURE SPIRITUAL WELL-BEING

1. 1 Thessalonians 4:13–18.

2. Matthew 7:24–25.

3. Matthew 7:12.

4. James 1:22.

5. Philippians 4:7.

6. Philippians 4:6.

7. 1 Peter 5:7.

8. Matthew 6:14.

9. 1 Corinthians 12:12–27.

10. Psalm 46:11.

11. Hebrews 11:6.

12. Daniel 2:20–23.

13. Psalm 150:2.

14. Joshua 1:8.

15. Psalm 48:9.

16. Psalm 119:97–99.

17. Psalm 32:6.

18. Matthew 26:41.

19. 1 Thessalonians 5:17–18.

20. Philippians 4:6.

21. Dorothy Gay Vela, "The Role of Religion/Spirituality in Building Strong Families: Respondents' Perceptions" (Ph.D. diss., University of Nebraska, Lincoln, 1996).

22. Ephesians 4:26.

CHAPTER 6. STEP SIX ◆ LEARN TO COPE WITH STRESS AND CRISES

1. Romans 14:7.

2. Philippians 4:6–8.

3. Proverbs 15:13.

4. Proverbs 17:22.

5. Matthew 6:34.

6. Genesis 2:2–3.

7. Exodus 31:15.

8. Philippians 4:6.

9. Isaiah 41:10.

APPENDIX C. WHAT YOU, YOUR CHURCH, YOUR BUSINESS, AND YOUR COMMUNITY CAN DO FOR FAMILIES

1. N. Stinnett, & N. Stinnett, "Family Life Religious Education," in *Young Adult Religious Education*, ed. H. Atkinson (Birmingham, Ala.: Religious Education Press, 1995), 271–90; and R. Money, *Ministering to Families: A Positive Plan of Action* (Abilene, Tex.: Abilene Christian University Press, 1987).

2. Personal correspondence with Kimball Bullington.

3. G. R. Foster, *Family/School/Community Partnership: School as Family* (Tallahassee: Florida Department of Education; Division of Vocational, Adult, Community Education, 1991), 16.

4. D. P. Keating, "Adolescent Thinking," in *At the Threshold: Developing Adolescent*, ed. S. S. Feldman and G. R. Elliot (Cambridge, Mass.: Harvard University Press, 1990), 54–89.

5. Carnegie Council, *Great Transitions*, 67.

6. V. C. Strassburger, *Adolescents and the Media: Medical and Psychological Impact* (Newbury Park, Calif.: Sage, 1995).

7. Carnegie Council, *Great Transitions*.

8. Ibid.

APPENDIX D. MORE ABOUT THE FAMILY-STRENGTHS RESEARCH

1. Of course, this does not mean that single-parent families or couples without children cannot be good families. Later studies were conducted on single-parent families. This research on more than seven hundred of these families is explained in more detail in John DeFrain, Judy Fricke, & Julie Elmen, *On Our Own: A Single Parent's Survival Guide* (Lexington, Mass.: Lexington Books, 1987).

◆ BIBLIOGRAPHY ◆

This bibliography is a partial list of the publications, dissertations, and theses to come from this research. They are listed in chronological order, beginning with the most recent, within each section.

BOOKS

Stinnett, N., D. Hilliard, & N. Stinnett. *Marriage Success for You: Charting Your Marriage Destiny*. Montgomary, Ala.: Family Strengths Press, 1999.

Stinnett, N., & M. O'Donnell. *Good Kids*. New York: Doubleday, 1996.

Olson, D. H., & J. DeFrain. *Marriage and the Family: Systems, Diversity, and Strengths*. Mountain View, Calif.: Mayfield, 1996.

Stinnett, N., J. Walters, & N. Stinnett. *Relationships in Marriage and the Family*. New York: Macmillan, 1991.

DeFrain, J., J. Fricke, & J. Elmen. *On Our Own: A Single Parent's Survival Guide*. Lexington, Mass.: Lexington Books, 1987.

Van Zandt, S., H. Lingren, G. Rowe, P. Zeece, L. Kimmons, P. Lee, D. Shell, & N. Stinnett, eds. *Family Strengths 7: Vital Connections*. Lincoln: University of Nebraska Press, 1986.

Williams, R., H. Lingren, G. Rowe, S. Van Zandt, P. Lee, & N. Stinnett, eds. *Family Strengths 6: Enhancement of Interaction*. Lincoln: University of Nebraska Press, 1985.

Rowe, G., J. DeFrain, H. Lingren, R. MacDonald, N. Stinnett, S. Van Zandt, & R. Williams, eds. *Family Strengths 5: Continuity and Diversity*. Newton, Mass.: Education Development Center, 1984.

Stinnett, N., J. DeFrain, K. King, H. Lingren, S. Van Zandt, & R. Williams, eds. *Family Strengths 4: Positive Support Systems*. Lincoln: University of Nebraska Press, 1982.

Stinnett, N., J. DeFrain, K. King, P. Knaub, & G. Rowe, eds. *Family Strengths 3: Roots of Well-Being*. Lincoln: University of Nebraska Press, 1981.

Stinnett, N., B. Chesser, J. DeFrain, & P. Knaub, eds. *Family Strengths: Positive Models for Family Life*. Lincoln: University of Nebraska Press, 1980.

Stinnett, N., B. Chesser, J. DeFrain, eds. *Building Family Strengths: Blueprints for Action*. Lincoln: University of Nebraska Press, 1979.

PARTS OR CHAPTERS IN BOOKS

Stinnett, N., & N. Stinnett. "Search for Strong Families." In *Handbook of Family Religious Education*, edited by B. Neff & D. Ratcliff, 164–87. Birmingham, Ala.: Religious Education Press, 1995.

Stinnett, N., & N. Stinnett. "Family Life Religious Education." In *Handbook of Young Adult Religious Education*, edited by A. Atkinson, 271–90. Birmingham, Ala.: Religious Education Press, 1995.

Ammons, P., & N. Stinnett. "The Vital Marriage: A Closer Look." In *Continuity and Change in Marriage and Family*, edited by J. Veevers, 190–95. New York: Holt, Rinehart, and Winston, 1991.

Stinnett, N., & J. DeFrain. "The Healthy Family: Is It Possible?" In *The Second Handbook on Parent Education*, edited by M. Fine, 53–74. New York: Academic Press, 1989.

Stinnett, N. "Research on Strong Families." In *National Leadership Forum on Strong Families*, edited by G. Rekers. Ventura, Calif.: Regal Books, 1985.

Stinnett, N. "Strong Families: A Portrait." In *Prevention in Family Services: Approaches to Family Wellness*, edited by D. Mace, 27–38. Beverly Hills, Calif.: Sage, 1983.

JOURNAL ARTICLES

DeFrain, J., N. DeFrain, & J. Lepard. "Family Strengths and Challenges in the South Pacific: An Exploratory Study in Fiji." *International Journal of the Sociology of the Family* 24 (1994): 25–47.

DeFrain, J., & N. Stinnett. "Building on the Inherent Strengths of Families: A Positive Approach for Family Psychologists and Counselors." *Topics in Family Psychology and Counseling* 1 (1992): 15–26.

DeFrain, J. "The Qualities of Strong Families: A Primer for Unitarian-Universalists." *Unitarian Universalism, 1991: Selected Essays.* Boston: Unitarian Universalist Ministers Association.

DeFrain, J. "The Role of the Unitarian-Universalist Church in Building Family Strengths." *Journal of Liberal Religious Education* (Spring 1991): 9–26.

Wuerffel, J., J. DeFrain, & N. Stinnett. "How Strong Families Use Humor." *Family Perspective* 24 (1990): 129–41.

Abbott, D. A., & W. H. Meredith. "Characteristics of Strong Families: Perceptions of Ethnic Parents." *Home Economics Research Journal* 17 (1988): 140–47.

Brigman, K. L., J. Schons, & N. Stinnett. "Strengths of Families in a Society under Stress: A Study of Strong Families in Iraq." *Family Perspective* 20 (1986): 61–73.

Knaub, P. K. "Growing Up in a Dual-Career Family: The Children's Perceptions." *Family Relations* 35 (1986): 431–37.

Knaub, P. K. "Professional Women Perceive Family Strengths." *Journal of Home Economics* (Summer 1985): 52–55.

Stinnett, N., D. Tucker, R. Smith, & D. Shell. "Executive Families: Strengths, Stresses, and Loneliness." *Wellness Perspectives* 2 (1985): 21–30.

Porter, R. W., N. Stinnett, P. Lee, R. Williams, & K. Townley, "Strengths of Russian Emigrant Families." *Wellness Perspectives* (Summer 1985).

Stinnett, N., D. Lynn, L. Kimmons, S. Fuenning, & J. DeFrain. "Family Strengths and Personal Wellness." *Wellness Perspectives* 1 (1984): 25–31.

Knaub, P., S. Hanna, & N. Stinnett. "Strengths of Remarried Families." *Journal of Divorce* 7 (1984): 41–55.

Casas, C., N. Stinnett, J. DeFrain, R. Williams, & P. Lee. "Latin American Family Strengths." *Family Perspective* 18 (1984): 11–17.

Stevenson, P., P. Lee, N. Stinnett, & J. DeFrain. "Family Commitment-Building Mechanisms and Family Functionality." *Family Perspective* 17 (1983): 175–80.

Stevenson, P., N. Stinnett, J. DeFrain, & P. Lee. "Family Commitment and Marital Need Satisfaction." *Family Perspective* 16 (1982): 157–64.

Stinnett, N., G. Sanders, J. DeFrain, & A. Parkhurst. "A Nationwide Study of Families Who Perceived Themselves as Strong." *Family Perspective* 16 (1982): 15–22.

Stinnett, N., B. Knorr, J. DeFrain, & G. Rowe. "How Strong Families Cope with Crises." *Family Perspective* 15 (1981): 159–66.

Ammons, P., & N. Stinnett. "The Vital Marriage: A Closer Look." *Family Relations* 19 (1980): 37–42.

Stinnett, N. "Strengthening Families." *Family Perspective* 13 (1979): 3–9.

Stinnett, N., & K. Sauer. "Relationship Patterns among Strong Families." *Family Perspective* 11 (1977): 3–11.

POPULAR AND EXTENSION PUBLICATIONS

Hoyt, C. "Seven Secrets of Happy Families." *McCall's*, December 1994, 98–100.

Stinnett, N. "Why Farm Families Are Happier." *Progressive Farmer*, August 1990, 18–21.

DeFrain, J., & N. Stinnett. "Strong Families and Strong Farming Organizations: Is There a Connection?" University of Nebraska Experiment Station Journal Series, 1989.

Stinnett, N. "Building Strong Families." In "My Thoughts" column, *Progressive Farmer*, April 1989.

Stinnett, N., & J. DeFrain. "Six Secrets of Strong Families." *Reader's Digest*, November 1987, 132–35.

Milofsky, D. "What Makes Happy Families?" *Redbook*, August 1981, 58–62.

Olds, S. "Do You Have What It Takes to Make a Good Marriage?" *Ladies Home Journal*, October 1980, 76–78, 202, 204.

Daly, R. "Building Family Strengths" (HEG 78-97). Cooperative Extension Service, Institute of Agriculture and Natural Resources, 1978.

Daly, R. "4-H Family Project—Building Family Strengths" (ED. 23-20-78). C.E.S., Cooperative Extension Service, Institute of Agriculture and Natural Resources, 1978.

DISSERTATIONS AND THESES

Boytim, D. C. "Perceptions of Southern Rural Adolescents Concerning Their Family Strengths." Master's thesis, University of Alabama, Tuscalousa, 1997.

Xie, X. "Strengths and Challenges of Chinese Families in Urban and Rural Areas." Ph.D. diss., University of Nebraska, Lincoln, 1994.

Jittrapanun, A. "Adolescent Wellness and Family Strengths in Thailand." Master's thesis, University of Alabama, Tuscaloosa, 1994.

Skoglund, K. "Adolescent Wellness among Southern Rural Adolescents." Master's thesis, University of Alabama, Tuscaloosa, 1992.

Chae, G. "Adolescent Well-Being and Family Strengths in Korea." Master's thesis, University of Alabama, Tuscaloosa, 1989.

Chen, Y. "Strengths of Chinese Families Who Have Immigrated to the United States." Master's thesis, University of Nebraska, Lincoln, 1988.

Collins, O. P. "Life Skills Development through 4-H: A Survey of Adolescent Attitudes." Master's thesis, University of Nebraska, Lincoln, 1984.

Johnson, S. "The Effects of Marriage Enrichment on Marital Adaptability, Cohesion and Family Strengths." Ph.D. diss., University of Nebraska, Lincoln, 1984.

Stoll, B. "Family Strengths in Austria, Germany, and Switzerland." Master's thesis, University of Nebraska, Lincoln, 1984.

Weber, V. P. "The Strengths of Black Families in Soweto, Johannesburg, South Africa." Master's thesis, University of Nebraska, Lincoln, 1984.

Lynn, W. D. "Leisure Activities in High-Strength, Middle-Strength, and Low-Strength Families." Ph.D. diss., University of Nebraska, Lincoln, 1983.

Rampey, T. S. "Religiosity, Purpose in Life, and Other Factors Related to Family Success: A National Study." Ph.D. diss., University of Nebraska, Lincoln, 1983.

Smith, R. C. "The Family Life of Executives: A Descriptive Study." Master's thesis, University of Nebraska, Lincoln, 1983.

Fricke, J. M. "Coping As Divorced Fathers and Mothers: A Nationwide Study of Sole, Joint and Split Custody." Master's thesis, University of Nebraska, Lincoln, 1982.

Simon, K. W. "Fatherhood in the Middle Years." Master's thesis, University of Nebraska, Lincoln, 1982.

Elmen, J. "Sole Custody and Joint Custody: A Nationwide Assessment of Divorced Parents and Children." Master's thesis, University of Nebraska, Lincoln, 1981.

Luetchens, M. "An Analysis of Some Characteristics of Strong Families and the Effectiveness of Marriage and Family Life Education." Ph.D. diss., University of Nebraska, Lincoln, 1981.

Porter, R. W. "Family Strengths of Russian Emigrants." Master's thesis, University of Nebraska, Lincoln, 1981.

Weber, W. C. "Families Cope with Stress: A Study of Family Strengths in Families Where a Spouse Has End-Stage Renal Disease." Ph.D. diss., University of Nebraska, Lincoln, 1981.

Gutz, G. K. T. "Couples' Enrichment: Program Development, Implementation, and Evaluation." Master's thesis, University of Nebraska, Lincoln, 1980.

King, J. "The Strengths of Black Families." Ph.D. diss., University of Nebraska, Lincoln, 1980.

Casas, C. "Relationship Patterns of Strong Families in Latin America." Master's thesis, University of Nebraska, Lincoln, 1979.

Sanders, G. F. "Family Strengths: A National Study." Master's thesis, University of Nebraska, Lincoln, 1979.

Strand, K. B. "Parent-Child Relationships among Strong Families." Master's thesis, University of Nebraska, Lincoln, 1979.

Leland, C. "The Relationship of Family Strengths to Personality Characteristics and Commitment." Ph.D. diss., Oklahoma State University, Stillwater, 1977.

Matthews, W. D. "Family Strengths, Commitment, and Religious Orientation." Master's thesis, Oklahoma State University, Stillwater, 1977.

McCumber, A. K. "Patterns of Dealing with Conflict in Strong Families." Ph.D. diss., Oklahoma State University, Stillwater, 1977.

Tomlinson, D. L. "Power Structure of Strong Families." Master's thesis, Oklahoma State University, Stillwater, 1977.

Wall, J. A. K. "Characteristics of Strong Families." Master's thesis, Oklahoma State University, Stillwater, 1977.

Ammons, P. W. "Vital-Total Marital Relationships among Strong Families and Their Association with Selected Demographic and Personality Variables." Ph.D. diss., Oklahoma State University, Stillwater, 1976.

Ball, O. L. "Communication Patterns in Strong Families." Master's thesis, Oklahoma State University, Stillwater, 1976.

Sauer, K. H. "Relationship Patterns of Strong Families." Master's thesis, Oklahoma State University, Stillwater, 1976.

Truitt, D. F. "Marital Need Satisfaction, Life Philosophies, and Personality Characteristics of Strong Families." Master's thesis, Oklahoma State University, Stillwater, 1976.

Stevenson, P. "Family Commitment: Application of a Theoretical Framework." Master's thesis, Oklahoma State University, Stillwater, 1975.

Wright, R. M. "The Manner in Which Strong Families Participate in Activities Which Comprise a Large Segment of Potential Family Interaction Time." Master's thesis, Oklahoma State University, Stillwater, 1975.